Computer Hacking

Other titles in Lucent's Crime Scene Investigations series include:

Computer Hacking

by Peggy J. Parks

LUCENT BOOKS
A part of Gale, Cengage Learning

GALE
CENGAGE Learning™

Detroit • New York • San Francisco • New Haven, Conn • Waterville, Maine • London

LIBRARY OF CONGRESS CATALOGING-IN-PUBLICATION DATA

Parks, Peggy J., 1951–
  Computer hacking / By Peggy J. Parks.
      p. cm. — (Crime scene investigations)
  Includes bibliographical references and index.
  ISBN 978-1-4205-0035-6 (hardcover)
  1. Computer crimes—Juvenile literature. 2. Computer crimes—Investigation—Juvenile literature. I. Title.
  HV6773.P376 2008
  363.25'968—dc22

                                                    2008016444

Lucent Books
27500 Drake Rd.
Farmington Hills, MI 48331

ISBN-13: 978-1-4205-0035-6
ISBN-10: 1-4205-0035-X

Printed in the United States of America
1 2 3 4 5 6 7 12 11 10 09 08

Contents

Foreword

The popularity of crime scene and investigative crime shows on television has come as a surprise to many who work in the field. The main surprise is the concept that crime scene analysts are the true crime solvers, when in truth, it takes dozens of people, doing many different jobs, to solve a crime. Often, the crime scene analyst's contribution is a small one. One Minnesota forensic scientist says that the public "has gotten the wrong idea. Because I work in a lab similar to the ones on *CSI*, people seem to think I'm solving crimes left and right—just me and my microscope. They don't believe me when I tell them that it's the investigators that are solving crimes, not me."

Crime scene analysts do have an important role to play, however. Science has rapidly added a whole new dimension to gathering and assessing evidence. Modern crime labs can match a hair of a murder suspect to one found on a murder victim, for example, or recover a latent fingerprint from a threatening letter, or use a powerful microscope to match tool marks made during the wiring of an explosive device to a tool in a suspect's possession.

Probably the most exciting of the forensic scientist's tools is DNA analysis. DNA can be found in just one drop of blood, a dribble of saliva on a toothbrush, or even the residue from a fingerprint. Some DNA analysis techniques enable scientists to tell with certainty, for example, whether a drop of blood on a suspect's shirt is that of a murder victim.

While these exciting techniques are now an essential part of many investigations, they cannot solve crimes alone. "DNA doesn't come with a name and address on it," says the Minnesota forensic scientist. "It's great if you have someone in custody to match the sample to, but otherwise, it doesn't help.

That's the investigator's job. We can have all the great DNA evidence in the world, and without a suspect, it will just sit on the shelf. We've all seen cases with very little forensic evidence get solved by the resourcefulness of a detective."

While forensic specialists get the most media attention today, the work of detectives still forms the core of most criminal investigations. Their job, in many ways, has changed little over the years. Most cases are still solved through the persistence and determination of a criminal detective whose work may be anything but glamorous. Many cases require routine, even mind-numbing tasks. After the July 2005 bombings in London, for example, police officers sat in front of video players watching thousands of hours of closed-circuit television tape from security cameras throughout the city, and as a result were able to get the first images of the bombers.

The Lucent Books Crime Scene Investigations series explores the variety of ways crimes are solved. Titles cover particular crimes such as murder, specific cases such as the killing of three civil rights workers in Mississippi, or the role specialists such as medical examiners play in solving crimes. Each title in the series demonstrates the ways a crime may be solved, from the various applications of forensic science and technology to the reasoning of investigators. Sidebars examine both the limits and possibilities of the new technologies and present crime statistics, career information, and step-by-step explanations of scientific and legal processes.

The Crime Scene Investigations series strives to be both informative and realistic about how members of law enforcement—criminal investigators, forensic scientists, and others—solve crimes, for it is essential that student researchers understand that crime solving is rarely quick or easy. Many factors—from a detective's dogged pursuit of one tenuous lead to a suspect's careless mistakes to sheer luck to complex calculations computed in the lab—are all part of crime solving today.

"The Bad Guys Are Making a Lot of Money"

In June 2002 a British teenager named Joseph McElroy was at his computer using Deathserv, some software that he had created himself. His intent was to download films, music, and games from the Internet and then establish an online storage area with room enough to store all the files he had downloaded. In order to accomplish that, he needed to access a highly advanced and powerful network with a huge amount of bandwidth. He chose the Fermi National Accelerator Lab (or Fermilab), one of the world's leading centers for research on high-energy physics and nuclear energy. McElroy knew he would have no trouble breaking into the Fermilab network because he had designed Deathserv to bypass electronic security systems.

Once McElroy had hacked in, he began to download and store hundreds of gigabytes of copyrighted files. He then sectioned off certain areas and password-protected them so he and his friends could access the files whenever they wanted. McElroy and his buddies had no idea what kind of network they had broken into—nor did they know that when their hacking caused the Fermilab computer system to slow down suspiciously to a crawl, technicians feared that the network had been breached by terrorists and "pressed the panic button."[1] The U.S. Department of Energy (DOE) sounded a full-scale nuclear terrorism alert and shut the entire computer system down for three days. The DOE notified London's Scotland Yard, and British law enforcement officers tracked McElroy to his home and arrested him.

McElroy faced the possibility of a long prison sentence and thousands of dollars in fines. Fortunately for him, his only punishment was two hundred hours of community service and a stern scolding by Judge Andrew Goymer. The judge stated that he did not think prison was necessary because of McElroy's good character and the fact that no actual harm was done. Security professional David Williamson later stated that he disagreed with the judge's light sentence: "The McElroy hacking case highlights an increasingly common practice in the online world. . . . Hacking is still illegal and as a self-confessed serial hacker, McElroy and the hacker community at large will view this outcome as a green light to break the law."[2]

High-Tech Crimes

Although McElroy's hacking job caused a great deal of panic, there was no real damage as a result of what he had done. But many other hacking cases involve sophisticated, serious crimes that leave catastrophe in their wake. Hackers have committed

Many computer hackers are young males who enjoy hacking for the thrill of overcoming the challenges of sophisticated online security.

fraudulent stock transactions, stolen Social Security numbers and credit card numbers, and spread viruses and other malicious software (known as malware) that infects entire computer systems. In August 2007 computer hackers attacked the Bank of India, one of the country's leading financial institutions, by imbedding malware into the HTML programming code of the bank's main Web site. When people visited it, they were silently redirected to a hacker site, where at least a dozen malware programs were installed on their computers. Then they were directed back to the Bank of India's site, unaware that their computers had been infected.

Hackers have also been known to steal user names and passwords and then use the information to withdraw money from accounts in banks and other financial institutions. In October 2006 a Wisconsin man named Dave DeSmidt was the victim of computer hacking—and he nearly lost the savings that he had built over twenty-five years. DeSmidt had $179,000 in his retirement account with the firm J.P. Morgan. Someone hacked into his account and, with a few clicks, ordered all the money to be transferred electronically to a private checking account at a bank. DeSmidt had no idea it had happened until he checked his balance and was shocked to see that it was $0. After a long investigation, DeSmidt's money was finally recovered and returned to his retirement account. But he says it was an extremely frightening and stressful time for him and his wife.

"The Problems Are Not Getting Solved"

Incidents such as DeSmidt's are becoming more and more prevalent as the number of hacking-related incidents continues to grow. One reason for this growth is the increasing presence of secretive online forums where hackers exchange ideas and learn from each other. Security expert Mark Rasch explains: "Information about hacking, cracking, and attacking is freely available. There are some 30,000 hacker-related Web sites on the Internet, and even more active bulletin board and newsgroup sites. The number of attacks and their costs go up every year. To date, more than 50,000 computer viruses have been created, and up to 400 are active at any one time."[3]

Computer hacking is a threatening problem all over the world. As hackers continue to develop more sophisticated techniques, the stakes will get higher and the risk will become even greater. As Internet security expert Gadi Evron explains: "I hate to scare people, but there is never 100 percent (security). . . . The problems are not getting solved. They are getting worse. The bad guys are making a lot of money."[4]

CHAPTER 1

The Growing Threat of Cybercrime

When the term *computer hacking* is used nowadays, it usually refers to malicious behavior and activities that are illegal and destructive. Stories appear in the news every day, describing how hackers have crashed computer systems, defaced Web sites, spread viruses, and created untold problems for millions of people all over the world. But the original meaning of hacking had nothing to do with damage or crime, and the original hackers did not have destruction on their minds.

In the early 1960s the hacker community sprang to life in the computer labs of the Massachusetts Institute of Technology (MIT) and other universities. A group of MIT graduate students, who were members of the Tech Model Railroad Club, used their technical skills to alter, or hack, electric trains and switches to make them perform better and faster. They were so fascinated with the school's enormous mainframe computers that they often snuck into the labs at night to examine the machines and see how they worked. These were the very first hackers, "computer nerds" who were motivated by interest and curiosity—and they were not afraid to sidestep rules and boundaries in order to find out what they wanted to know. Renowned computer hacker Richard Stallman says that what all the original hackers had in common was a "spirit of playful cleverness," and that they typically had "little respect for the silly rules that administrators like to impose, so they looked for ways around." The hackers prided themselves in finding ways to bypass the computers' security restrictions. Part of their reason for doing this, says Stallman, was "so they could use the computers freely, and partly just for the sake of cleverness (hacking does not need to be useful)."[5]

Well-known hacker Richard Stallman speaks at a press conference in 2000. Stallman and others like him consider themselves legitimate hackers.

"Monstrous Levels of Crime"

There are still many hackers who fit Stallman's description. Thinking of themselves as "legitimate hackers," they become frustrated when the term *hacker* is used by the media to describe people who use computers to commit crimes or cause destruction. They say that such criminals are thugs who should be called crackers, rather than hackers. But as technical writer Andrew Brandt explains, the terms are often used interchangeably: "Whether you call them hackers, crackers, or computer-vredebreuk (Dutch for 'disturbers of the peace of a computer'),

there's no doubt that as long as computing systems exist, people will be looking for—and finding—ways to break into them."[6]

No matter what they are called, the motives of many hackers have radically changed from what they used to be. Today's criminal hackers are not driven by curiosity, nor is their goal to better understand the inner workings of computers. Instead, they use their knowledge and technical skills to commit serious crimes and victimize businesses, government agencies, financial organizations, and consumers throughout the world. Tim Rosenberg, a research professor at George Washington University, describes how prevalent this cybercrime has become: "This is not about little Jimmy Smith breaking into his ex-employer's website and selling information to competitors. What we're seeing is just sheer, monstrous levels of crime."[7]

According to a 2007 State of the Net survey by *Consumer Reports*, American consumers lost more than $7 billion between 2005 and 2006 because of hacking-related crimes. Yet many security experts say it is nearly impossible to determine accurately the scope and extent of hacking crimes. According to Carl Livitt, a network security manager with Agenda Security, one major problem is that an alarming number of companies do not even know if their computer systems are secure, nor are they always aware when those systems have been hacked. During investigations performed by Agenda Security in 2006, security analysts were able to gain some form of access to their clients' networks, and their presence was unknown until they showed the reports to clients.

As hackers become more sophisticated and the number of cybercrimes continues to skyrocket, putting a stop to computer hacking is an enormous challenge for law enforcement officials. Hackers know everything about how computers work, and they are amazingly tech-savvy—often much more so than the people who are trying to catch them. In addition to knowing how to crack through security systems, they know how to cover their tracks, which makes it extremely difficult for them to be caught. Security expert Yohai Einav explains: "Chasing these . . . fraudsters is like chasing terrorists in Afghanistan.

The Famous Phone Phreak

In the early 1970s a hacker named John Draper learned that a toy whistle inside Cap'n Crunch cereal generated the same high-pitched tone as AT&T's long-distance switching system. That was the beginning of phreaking, which involved breaking into the telephone network to obtain free long-distance service. Draper, who became known as Cap'n Crunch, gives his account of the experience:

With this whistle, it was possible to access the internal trunking mechanism of Ma Bell [telephone company]. In conjunction with a blue box (a special tone generating device), it was possible to take internal control of Ma Bell's long distance switching equipment. . . . Naturally, neither the phone companies or the authorities took kindly to my blue box "experiments" I was performing on their equipment, so they tracked me down and filed charges, convicting me under Title 18, Section 1343 : Fraud by wire.

After Draper was convicted of wire fraud charges in 1976, he was arrested twice more in 1978 and 1979, and he served time for all three offenses. Since then he has given numerous presentations on computer security issues and also created a highly advanced firewall for computers known as CrunchBox.

John T. Draper, "The Story So Far," Cap'n Crunch in Cyberspace, 2005. www.webcrunchers.com/crunch/story.html.

You know they are somewhere out there, but finding their caves, their underground bunkers, is almost impossible."[8]

The WhiteHat Team

One notorious hacker is a Romanian man named Victor Faur, the leader of a hacking gang called the WhiteHat Team. In 2006 Faur was indicted by a federal grand jury for hacking into more than 150 government computers in the United States, including machines at the National Aeronautics and Space Administration's (NASA's) Jet Propulsion Laboratory and Goddard Space Flight Center; the Sandia National Laboratories in Albuquerque, New Mexico; and the U.S. Naval Observatory in Washington, D.C. According to government reports, the WhiteHat Team's reason for choosing these computers was to prove their ability to hack into systems that were thought to be some of the most secure in the world. Their hacking operation reportedly went on for about two years before they were caught.

Prosecutors say that once Faur hacked into the computers and took control of them, he bragged about his accomplishment to users by causing the machines "to display screens that flaunted the computer intrusion."[9] In addition, Faur configured the computers to perform as chat rooms, where he could communicate with other members of the WhiteHat Team. Government sources also say that Faur searched the computers for passwords that he could use to gain unauthorized access to other computers.

The systems that were hacked by Faur and his group were critical for government operations. They were used to collect and process data from spacecraft orbiting Earth and in deep space; to collect, store, and analyze scientific data; and to evaluate new scientific technologies. Once the hacking was discovered, the U.S. Energy Department, NASA, and the U.S. Navy grew concerned that they could not trust the integrity of the data on the computers that had been compromised. As a result, entire systems had to be rebuilt, and while the computers were offline, scientists and engineers had to communicate manually with spacecraft. All in all, the government organizations that were hacked suffered approximately $1.5 million in losses. If Faur is extradited to the United States from Romania, he faces up to fifty-four years in federal prison for his crimes.

Identity Theft

As costly and foolhardy as the WhiteHat Team's hacking job was, their motives could be considered malicious mischief, rather than hard-core cybercrime. But that is not the case with many hacking jobs, which can result in disastrous circumstances for unsuspecting computer users. One of the most frightening types of hacking crimes is identity theft, or the act of stealing confidential information in order to assume someone's identity. According to the Gartner Group research firm, the rate of identity theft has jumped 50 percent since 2003, when the Federal Trade Commission estimated that more than 9 million Americans had been victimized. Based on an August 2006 study, Gartner analysts say that as many as 15 million Americans were victims of identity theft between 2005 and 2006. This sort of cybercrime is flourishing, as an article in *USA Today* states: "Criminals covet your identity data

Scientists and engineers were forced to communicate manually with spacecraft after hackers violated NASA's high-security computer systems.

like never before. What's more, they've perfected more ways to access your bank accounts, grab your Social Security number and manipulate your identity than you can imagine."[10]

Identity thieves are often brazen in their use of stolen data. They have been known to rent apartments under victims' names; open bank accounts and write bad checks; obtain credit cards and loans and then run up balances without paying them; open accounts with cable TV, telephone, and other utility companies; and even get a job using someone else's Social Security number. Victims may have no idea that their identities have been stolen until they receive statements in the mail, review their credit reports, or are contacted by debt collectors or collection agencies. It can take months, or even years, to repair the damage to someone's name or credit rating caused by identity thieves. The Federal Trade Commission explains: "Some consumers victimized by identity theft may lose out on job opportunities, or be denied loans for education, housing or cars because of negative information on their credit reports. In rare cases, they may even be arrested for crimes they did not commit."[11]

During the summer of 2007 Joe Musich was shocked to learn that he was the victim of identity theft. The Littleton, Colorado, resident ordered a copy of his credit report. When he received it, he discovered that someone in California had been using his Social Security number and other personal information since 1995. The person, who went by the name of Jose Luna, had opened dozens of accounts and listed numerous different addresses, all of which appeared on Musich's credit report. As of November 2007 Musich remained unsure how much financial damage had been done, nor did he have any idea how long it would take him to clean up the mess that was created by the identity thief.

How Identity Thieves Work

The most common way that identity thieves steal personal information is through phishing, a type of Internet fraud that is designed to fish passwords, bank account and credit card numbers, Social Security numbers, and other personal data that are stored on computers. Phishing is a form of social engineering, meaning hackers use personalized methods in order to steal the information they want. Bogus e-mails are created so they appear to be from banks, credit card companies, government agencies, PayPal, and other providers. The e-mails tell users that there is a problem with their account and that the only way to fix it is to click a link in the e-mail and confirm passwords and other confidential information. People respond because they do not realize the e-mails are fraudulent—and if they provide the requested information, they are handing it over to criminals.

> **By the Numbers**
>
> **$67 BILLION**
>
> **The FBI's estimate of what American businesses lost in 2006 due to computer-related crimes.**

Spearphishing is the most sophisticated form of social engineering. Whereas ordinary phishing attempts can involve thousands, or even millions, of e-mails that are sent out randomly, spearphishing is a much more targeted attack. E-mails are sent to a select group of people and often appear to come from a trusted person or authority figure, such as an employer. Hackers craft the e-mails in such a way that they are very convincing, and because they are personalized, they often catch people unaware. If people fall for the scam, they end up on Web sites that are designed to snatch confidential information.

Identity thieves also use other methods of tricking people into visiting malicious sites. In November 2007 security officials discovered that hackers were using major search engines such as Google to lure unsuspecting users to these sites. When terms as common as "Christmas gifts," "hospice," or "how to teach a dog to play fetch" were typed in, results appeared on the first screen that seemed to be legitimate—but anyone who fell for

E-mail scams known as phishing are an easy way for hackers to glean information from unsuspecting computer users.

the trick and clicked into the booby-trapped sites was at risk of having confidential information snatched.

Hack, Pump, and Dump

Many identity theft schemes are carried out by sophisticated international crime rings, such as a gang of hackers who stole money from American brokerage firms between July and November 2006. The hackers were Indian men who operated out of Thailand and India and ran a stock fraud operation known to security officials as "hack, pump, and dump." First they used their own personal brokerage accounts to purchase thousands of shares of various stocks. Then, using stolen user names and passwords, they hacked into customers' online accounts at well-known brokerage firms such as Merrill Lynch, Charles Schwab, TD Ameritrade, and Fidelity Brokerage Services. The men used funds in the accounts to make large purchases of the same stocks they had previously bought—which drove up the market price to more than nine times its average value. Once the share prices were artificially inflated, the hackers sold their own stocks at the higher prices, and they netted profits of more than $121,000. According to the Securities and Exchange Commission, the criminals' actions caused nearly $900,000 in damage to brokerage firm customers. One victim had $180,000 in investments; when he returned from a five-day fishing trip in Alaska, he was horrified to discover that his balance was negative $200,000.

After a lengthy investigation by law enforcement officials, the criminals' illegal actions were discovered. Two out of three were captured in Hong Kong in early 2007, marking the first time that hackers had ever been arrested overseas for an online attack on American brokerage firms. According to security expert Paul Moriarty, this case is an example of how clever cybercriminals have become in hacking through computer security systems. He explains: "These aren't social misfits operating from Mom's house. These are people who are really going after this to try and make money."[12]

ShadowCrew

Another notorious hacking gang evaded law enforcement for two years before they were caught. The gang, known as ShadowCrew, was founded in 2002 by Andrew Mantovani of Scottsdale, Arizona, and David Appleyard of Linwood, New Jersey. ShadowCrew hackers obtained hundreds of thousands of credit card numbers through phishing e-mails, as well as by hacking into databases to steal account data. Security officials say the gang cracked the networks of at least twelve companies that were not even aware their systems had been breached.

On Sunday nights, members congregated at the ShadowCrew Web site. It served as a forum where they shared tips with each other about fraudulent acts such as how to create convincing phishing e-mails and fake IDs. It was also an online auction where members could buy and sell stolen credit card and bank account numbers, as well as fake driver's licenses, passports, and birth certificates. In May

Brandon Monchamp, shown here, was a member of the notorious ShadowCrew gang. ShadowCrew made millions of dollars by identity theft.

2004 a ShadowCrew hacker known as Scarface sold 115,695 credit card numbers in just a single transaction with another member.

In an October 2004 sting known as Operation Firewall, Secret Service agents arrested twenty-eight members of ShadowCrew from the United States and six other countries. Christopher Christie, one of the U.S. attorneys who prosecuted the ShadowCrew case, explains the importance of the arrest. "These individuals operated a virtual trading post for stolen identity and financial information. They were international in their reach and we are pleased to say they are out of business. We look forward to hunting down and prosecuting more operators like them to spare consumers the nightmare of identify theft."[13] By the time ShadowCrew was caught, the gang had allegedly made more than $4.3 million in illegal profits from stolen credit cards.

Attack of the Iceman

A renowned hacker named Max Ray Butler also founded an online forum that was a massive identity theft operation—but he took ShadowCrew's criminal activities to a much higher level. Butler, an expert hacker and former security consultant who used online names such as Iceman, Digits, and Aphex, used wireless access points to break into multiple computer networks of financial institutions and credit card processing firms. He then stole credit card numbers and other personal information, which he peddled on a Web site he had created called CardersMarket. In order to expand his criminal activities and create a megaforum, Butler staged a deliberate takeover of four rival sites during August 2006. The rival forums were DarkMarket, TalkCash, ScandinavianCarding, and TheVouched.

After Butler hacked into the sites' databases, he extracted their combined forty-five hundred members, thereby quadrupling CardersMarket's membership to six thousand. Security expert Dan Clements says that Butler created "the Wal-Mart of the underground. Anything you need to commit your crimes, you can get in his forum."[14] Soon after the takeover, Butler sent an e-mail to all new members, touting CardersMarket's superiority over every other forum. He also announced that the site's host computer had been moved to Iran, which put it beyond the reach of law enforcement officials in the United States.

As safe as he believed himself to be, however, Butler was finally tracked down by the FBI. He was arrested in September 2007 and indicted for three counts of wire fraud and two counts of transferring stolen identity information. If he is convicted of all charges, he faces up to forty years in prison and $1.5 million in fines.

A Staggering Loss

Unfortunately for consumers, though, many other criminal hacking gangs have managed to avoid being caught. As of December 2007 law enforcement officials had still not tracked down hackers who were responsible for a massive security breach of TJX Companies that occurred during 2005 and 2006. TJX, which runs more than 2,500 retail stores worldwide, including T.J. Maxx, HomeGoods, and Marshalls, keeps a massive database of customer credit and debit card numbers. The heist remained undetected for eighteen months. By the time it was discovered, criminal hackers had stolen and sold off the numbers of nearly 100 million consumers in thirteen countries, including at least 29 million MasterCard and 65 million Visa numbers.

The data security management firm Protegrity estimates that the losses from the TJX security breach were as high as

$1.6 billion; but because the criminals have not been caught and the stolen numbers are still out there, the total losses will likely continue to climb. "These guys perpetrated a perfect crime," says security professional Ken Steinberg. "This is what scares the living daylights out of everybody. And this one won't be the last."[15] Security experts say that the TJX breach was the biggest theft of personal data ever recorded.

"The Baddest of the Bad"

An international crime ring known as the Russian Business Network (RBN) has also avoided capture. The RBN is a worldwide hub for Web sites specifically devoted to criminal activities such as identity theft, spamming, extortion, and child pornography. It is based in St. Petersburg, Russia, and offers Web site hosting—often at rates that are ten times higher than those of legitimate hosts—to people who are actively engaged in criminal activities. RBN ensures its customers that their sites are "bullet-proof," meaning that they will remain accessible on the Internet even if law enforcement officials try to shut them down.

RBN is a shadowy operation that officials at VeriSign, one of the largest security firms in the world, calls "the baddest of the bad."[16] The group is difficult for law enforcement officials to catch because it has no legal identity, is not registered as a company, has no official Web site of its own, and registers its domains to anonymous addresses. In addition, RBN does not advertise to attract customers. Anyone who wants to use its services must make contact through Internet instant-messaging services or through secretive Russian online forums. Interested parties must prove to RBN that they are not working undercover for law enforcement, often by demonstrating active involvement in cybercrime that involves stealing financial and personal data. Once customers' identities have been established, they are required to pay for their Web site hosting with untraceable electronic funds.

Recent reports by VeriSign and other security firms indicate that crime rings operating through RBN's computer network

Becoming a Computer Security Specialist

Job Description:

Computer security specialists are responsible for maintaining computer systems to protect data from unauthorized users. These highly skilled professionals build secure infrastructures to guard against infiltration of malicious software and system crashes, assess the vulnerabilities of their systems, keep security procedures updated, and conduct regular investigations to verify levels of compliance with security policies. They also play the role of detective, researching the latest computer threats and developing strategies to respond.

Education:

Most computer security specialists hold bachelor's or master's degrees in computer science or a related field, but it is their knowledge, experience, and technical expertise that employers value most. They often take courses in computer security, as well as study hacking techniques, so they are better prepared to protect their own systems.

Qualifications:

Although certification is not required by most organizations, many security specialists choose to become certified by agencies such as the International Information Systems Security Certifications Consortium or the Institute for Certification of Computer Experts.

Additional Information:

Besides technical expertise, computer security specialists need excellent problem-solving and strategic-thinking skills; must be able to communicate and listen well, work independently, and write clear, concise reports; and have a positive attitude and strong work ethic.

Salary:

From $80,000 to over $110,000 per year.

are responsible for a large portion of the world's cybercrime. That includes about half of the phishing incidents that occurred during 2006. Security experts say that one of RBN's most ruthless customers is Rock Phish, a notorious gang of hackers that has victimized customers of financial institutions in the United States and Europe. In a 2006 phishing scheme, Rock Phish used RBN's network to steal more than $150 million. In November 2007 Websense Security Labs discovered that Rock Phish was sending out HTML e-mails to people, inviting them to view a video on the video site YouTube. Once they clicked the URL and entered the site, they were directed to a bogus page that resembled the real YouTube. A message popped up saying that the video could not load and attempted to trick users into downloading a Flash player. If they did, malware was installed on their computers that allowed the hackers to steal personal information. According to Symantec security expert Zulfikar Ramzan, Rock Phish is "the major driving force behind a worsening situation, and they are difficult to track down."[17]

"There's No End in Sight"

Whether they operate out of Russia, India, the United States, or anywhere else in the world, computer hackers present a massive threat. Growing numbers of hackers are criminals who are ruthless in their attacks on computer systems and their pursuit of confidential information that will help them steal identities and commit other fraudulent acts. Because they are tech-savvy experts, many of them are able to commit their crimes without being caught by law enforcement. According to security experts, this problem will continue to grow worse in the years to come, as the security firm McAfee explains: "Cyber crime is a grim reality that's growing at an alarming rate, and no one is immune to the mounting threat. It is costing consumers, businesses, and nations billions of dollars annually, and there's no end in sight."[18]

"It Was Like a Game"

When the book *The Hacker's Handbook* was published in Great Britain in 1985, it became an influential guide for aspiring computer hackers. In the introduction, author Hugo Cornwall referred to hacking as a "recreational and educational sport" and defined it as follows:

> [Hacking] consists of attempting to make unauthorised entry into computers and to explore what is there. The sport's aims and purposes have been widely misunderstood; most hackers are not interested in perpetrating massive frauds, modifying their personal banking, taxation and employee records, or inducing one world superpower into inadvertently commencing Armageddon in the mistaken belief that another super-power is about to attack it. Every hacker I have ever come across has been quite clear about where the fun lies: it is in developing an understanding of a system and finally producing the skills and tools to defeat it. In the vast majority of cases, the process of "getting in" is much more satisfying than what is discovered in the protected computer files.[19]

Cornwall's book had a powerful effect on Gary McKinnon, a Scottish teenager who lived with his family in England. McKinnon says the book was his main inspiration to become a hacker, which he eventually did—and by 2002 the U.S. government was calling him "the biggest military computer hack of all time."[20]

Fascination with UFOs

McKinnon's primary reason for wanting to hack was so he could access information on a topic that was of great interest to

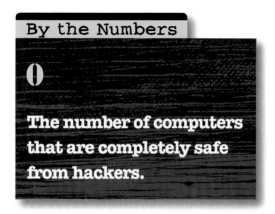

0

The number of computers that are completely safe from hackers.

him: unidentified flying objects (UFOs). He believed that the best place to find UFO data was in the computers of government agencies, because he was convinced that information was being concealed from the public. He first started exploring the systems in 1995. First he downloaded a program that would scan the computers of government and military organizations in the United States. It did not take him long to find holes in the systems, such as user names that were not supported by passwords. He used that information to hack into the computers and start snooping.

For the next seven years, McKinnon (known as Solo) continued to hack into high-level networks, including the U.S. Department of Defense; the Army, Navy, and Air Force; and NASA. He became so obsessed with hacking that he quit his job as a systems administrator for a small business. He rarely left the house he shared with his girlfriend, stopped eating proper meals, and did not even shower or bother to change out of his pajamas. "It was like a game," he says. "I loved computer games. I still do. It was like a real game. It was addictive. Hugely addictive."[21] McKinnon says that while he was inside the government's computer systems, there were as many as seventy other hackers in the network at the same time, looking at the data along with him. When he examined their IP addresses, he saw that they were from Denmark, Italy, Germany, Turkey, China, and Thailand, as well as other countries.

According to McKinnon, he made some fascinating discoveries during his years of hacking. He claims that in NASA's files there were huge photographs of UFOs that had been taken by satellites, including one that was distinctly alien looking, a "silvery, cigar-shaped object with geodesic spheres on either side. . . . The object didn't look manmade or anything like what we have created."[22] He also allegedly found an Excel spreadsheet that was titled "Non-Terrestrial Officers." The document, according to McKinnon, contained names and ranks of U.S. Air Force officers who were not registered anywhere else. That, he says, was an indication that the Americans had a secretive base where these officers were stationed—and it was somewhere out in space, rather than on Earth.

McKinnon was arrested in 2002 by the British National High-Tech Crime Unit, and he says that it was somewhat of a relief: "I think I almost wanted to be caught, because it was ruining me. I had this classic thing of wanted to be caught so there would be an end to it."[23] Officers confiscated McKinnon's computers and kept him in custody for several hours. After he admitted to unlawfully accessing computers, he was released and told that his punishment would likely be community service. But on November 12, 2002, the U.S. Department of Justice indicted McKinnon on seven counts of computer fraud and stated its intent to formally request that the British government extradite

Gary McKinnon, far right, speaks after his extradition hearing in London. McKinnon hacked into sensitive U.S. military computer systems for his own enjoyment.

him. As of December 2007 he was still uncertain of his fate. If he is extradited to the United States, tried, and found guilty, he faces imprisonment for up to forty years and $1.75 million in fines.

The First Cyber Bank Robber

About the time that McKinnon was just starting to hack computers, an expert hacker from Russia was in the midst of a massive theft operation. Vladimir Levin was the leader of a notorious hacking gang. During the summer of 1994, he became the first person to hack into a bank's computer system to steal money—and in doing so, he committed one of the biggest bank robberies of all time.

Working late at night to avoid suspicion, Levin used a computer terminal at AO Saturn, a computer company located in St. Petersburg, Russia, to hack into the computer network of New York–based Citibank. He used stolen user names and passwords to withdraw money gradually from Citibank accounts. Over the next several months, Levin and his accomplices transferred more than $10 million to accounts at financial institutions throughout the world, including Finland, Israel, Germany, Switzerland, and the United States.

In August 1994 Citibank detected two suspicious transfers that totaled nearly $400,000. Bank officials alerted the FBI, which began to track and analyze the bank's online transactions. This investigation led them to Levin. On March 3, 1995, British law enforcement officials arrested him at Stansted Airport in London as he was about to change planes. Although he fought extradition for two years, Levin lost his case and in September 1997 was delivered to the United States for trial. He pleaded guilty in federal court to charges of conspiracy

By the Numbers

217 MILLION

The number of U.S. residents' data records that have been exposed due to security breaches since January 2005.

The notorious computer hacker Kevin Mitnick is arrested in 1995. After prison, Mitnick became a "white hat hacker."

to commit bank, wire, and computer fraud. In February 1998 a federal judge sentenced Levin to three years in prison and ordered him to pay Citibank more than $240,000.

"The World's Most Notorious Hacker"

Another hacker who served time in prison was Kevin Mitnick, who was known on the Internet as Condor. Mitnick's interest in computer hacking actually evolved from his fascination with magic. As a boy growing up in Southern California, he spent weekends hanging out in magic shops because he wanted to learn the secrets of how magicians performed their tricks. He explains how that interest eventually led to hacking: "Once I learned how a new trick worked, I would practice, practice, and practice until I mastered it. To an extent it was through magic that I discovered the enjoyment in fooling people."[24]

Mitnick's first tricks started when was a teenager and became intrigued with telephones and the inner workings of their electronics and switching systems. He taught himself the skill of phone phreaking, which allowed him to gain unauthorized access to telephone switches and make long-distance calls, as well as change someone's class of service. As one of his pranks, Mitnick rigged the phone system so that whenever his friend tried to make a telephone call from home, a voice came on the line asking him to deposit ten cents, as though he were using a pay phone.

By the time Mitnick was in high school, he was a full-fledged hacker. A group of fellow hackers dared him to break into a Digital Equipment Corporation computer system called The Ark, and he had no problem proving that he could do it. He also hacked into the networks of Motorola Corporation and Nokia; compromised telephone switches in California, New York, Chicago, and Maryland; and eavesdropped on telephone lines at the U.S. National Security Agency. Eventually he was caught stealing technical manuals from the Pacific Bell telephone company, but his only punishment was probation. He violated it, however, by hacking into a university's computer system, so he was sentenced to six months in jail.

In December 1988 Mitnick was arrested again. This time he was charged with hacking into Digital Equipment Corporation's computer network and stealing software that the company said was worth $1 million. He later explained that even though what he did was wrong, his intent was never malicious; rather, his only motive for hacking was to build knowledge and hone his skills. "My misdeeds were motivated by curiosity," he says. "I wanted to know as much as I could about how phone networks worked, and the ins and outs of computer security. I went from being a kid who loved to perform magic tricks to becoming the world's most notorious hacker, feared by corporations and the government."[25]

Bad Guys Become Good Guys

Mitnick was convicted of computer fraud in 1989, and he went to prison for a year. After he got out and was nearing the end of his probationary period, he learned that the government was gathering evidence for another case against him. So he ran away and spent the next three years as a fugitive. He moved from city to city, often choosing his location based on *Money* magazine's reports on the best places to live in America. The whole time he was on the run, he continued to hack into computer networks using his laptop computer and cellular phone. In a July 4, 1994, front-page story in the *New York Times*, reporter John Markoff called Mitnick "cyberspace's most wanted," and "one of the nation's most wanted computer criminals."[26]

The 414 Gang

In August 1983 seven teenage boys from Milwaukee were caught by the FBI in one of the first major hacking sting operations. The hackers, who had met as members of a local Explorer Scout troop, had been getting together to use home computers and modems to hack into mainframe computers located throughout the United States and Canada. They started calling themselves the 414s, named after their city's telephone area code. The FBI tracked them down by tracing telephone calls they had made in order to access computer systems. By the time they were caught, the 414s had hacked into more than fifty computer systems, including a New Mexico nuclear research institution called the Los Alamos National Laboratory, New York's Memorial Sloan-Kettering Cancer Center, and Security Pacific National Bank. Their escapades gained national media publicity, including a front-page story in *Newsweek* magazine that featured the group's leader, Neal Patrick. For the first time, the word *hacker* was used to describe criminal actions.

In February 1995 the FBI tracked Mitnick to his apartment in Raleigh, North Carolina, and arrested him. At his hearing he was accused of hacking into numerous computer networks, including Motorola, Fujitsu, Nokia Mobile Phones, Sun Microsystems, U.S. West, Air Touch Cellular, MCI, Pacific Bell, Novell, NEC, and Colorado SuperNet. Prosecutors claimed that once he hacked into these systems, he stole proprietary software and caused millions of dollars in losses. He was convicted and sentenced to five years in Lompoc Federal Correctional Institution, followed by three years' probation. During most of his probation, he was not allowed to use computers, cell phones, or any other type of electronic equipment, with the exception of a common landline telephone.

Today Mitnick is known as a "white hat hacker." He owns his own security company and uses his knowledge and experience to educate others on security issues and the threat of computer hacking. "I like my life now," he says. "I made some really stupid mistakes in the past as a younger man that I regret. I'm lucky that I've been given a second chance and that I could use these skills to help the community."[27]

The Hacking Exploits of Dark Dante

Kevin Poulsen is another white hat hacker—and like Mitnick, he committed numerous computer crimes before turning his life around. By the time Poulsen was a teenager, he was known as a brilliant hacker. Using the screen name Dark Dante, he used his hacking skills to break into government and military computer systems that were thought to be completely secure. One system he hacked into was ARPANET, which was a product of the Department of Defense and the precursor to the Internet. Poulsen was caught in 1983, but because he was a juvenile, he was not charged with a crime. In fact, his hacking expertise landed him a dream job. SRI International, a research organization under contract with the U.S. government, hired him to test network security for the Pentagon.

Poulsen began living a double life. During the day he used his hacking skills legally in the course of performing his job. At night, however, his actions were criminal. In addition to being a hacker, he was an accomplished lock picker, and used his expertise to break into Pacific Bell offices to steal equipment and information that would help him once he hacked into the phone company's network. In November 1989 Poulsen was caught again and charged with conspiracy, fraud, and wiretapping. But before he could be tried for his crimes, he fled and managed to evade law enforcement officials for seventeen months.

While he was in hiding, Poulsen committed what many people say was his most infamous hacking job. A Los Angeles radio station held a contest, and one lucky listener had the chance to win a brand-new Porsche 944. After hearing three particular songs in a row, listeners were told to call the station and that the 102nd caller would win the car. Working with a friend, Poulsen hacked into the station's telephone system and took control of its twenty-five lines, thereby blocking people from being able to call in. Because he was the only person who could get through, he dialed the station's number over and over until he was the 102nd caller, and the Porsche was his.

Kevin Poulsen, shown here, went by the name Dark Dante during his hacking days. Now Poulsen is a senior editor for a computer magazine.

In April 1991 Poulsen was tracked down by the FBI and arrested on charges of telecommunications and computer fraud. He was convicted and sentenced to fifty-one months in prison, as well as ordered to pay more than fifty thousand dollars in fines. After his release in 1996, he had trouble finding a job because he was forbidden to use a computer for three years. He became a freelance writer specializing in articles about security and hacking. Today the former Dark Dante is a journalist and senior editor for *Wired News*.

The Malicious Mafiaboy

Like Poulsen and most other hackers, Mike Calce started breaking into computer systems at a young age. Calce, who was from Montreal, Canada, operated under the screen name Mafiaboy. As a teenager, he spent his nights hanging out in an Internet chat room where he talked with fellow hackers, often annoying them because he constantly bragged about his hacking "skilz."[28] Serious hackers believed that Calce was nothing more than one of the "script-kiddies," or immature teenagers who used limited hacking skills to engage in online vandalism. To them, people like Mafiaboy gave legitimate hackers a bad name.

Calce did not appreciate being rejected by the other hackers, so he decided to show what he could do. On the morning of February 7, 2000, the Internet site Yahoo.com was hit with a distributed denial-of-service (DDoS) attack, which means it was suddenly bombarded with massive amounts of data coming from the outside—the equivalent of 3.5 million e-mail messages every second. The flood of data caused the system to crash, and administrators frantically hunted for the glitch. It did not take them long to realize that it was not a normal system problem; rather, the site had been deliberately attacked. The next day, the Web sites Buy.com, eBay, and Amazon.com were also hit with DDoS attacks, and they, too, suffered significant service outages and delays.

FBI security official Bill Swallow was assigned to investigate the case, and he became an undercover monitor for the hacker chat room. On the evening of February 8, Mafiaboy was back in the online forum bragging that he was responsible for the DDoS attacks. Again, no one believed him, and one hacker scoffed that if Mafiaboy was really capable of all the feats he bragged about, maybe he should try hitting CNN. Mafiaboy took him up on it—and within minutes, the damage became apparent. Investigative reporter and author Dan Verton explains:

CNN's global online news operation, as well as 1,200 other Web sites that CNN hosted worldwide, started to grind to a crawl. By the following day, Datek and E-Trade, both online stock-trading companies, entered crisis mode as sporadic outages of Internet operations threatened the health of the financial markets. . . . This was a true crisis, the one that all of the experts had been warning about for years. . . . The FBI needed to find the hacker who called himself Mafiaboy. And they needed to find him fast.[29]

Calce was arrested on April 15, 2000, by the Royal Canadian Mounted Police. By that time, he was believed to have hacked into at least seventy-five computer systems in fifty-two networks throughout Canada, Korea, Denmark, and the United States, causing more than $1.5 million in damages. The following September, a Canadian judge sentenced Calce to spend eight months in a juvenile detention center. According to police inspector Yves Roussel, he was caught because he was unsophisticated and not good enough at hacking to cover his tracks. Roussel also says that hackers are, by nature, competitive with each other, and that Mafiaboy was clearly out of his league: "They want to show they're good at it and compete to be the best. Except Mafiaboy wasn't the best. He was not what we would call a genius in that field."[30]

Hacking's Boy Wonder

Ace hacker Jonathan "cOmrade" James was also a teenager when his hacking crimes were discovered. But unlike Mafiaboy, James ended up serving time in federal prison. When he was fifteen, he hacked into NASA's computer network and stole software, including some that was used in climate control operations for the International Space Station. He also hacked into the Department of Defense's network. One Department of Defense computer system belonged to the Defense Threat Reduction

Hacker Prank

On July 4, 1994, *New York Times* reporter John Markoff began a series of articles about Kevin Mitnick in which the superhacker was portrayed as a dangerous villain. Mitnick called Markoff's articles "outrageous lies," and said that they were influential in turning the public and law enforcement against him. "The power of one unethical reporter from such an influential newspaper to write a false and defamatory story about anyone should haunt each and every one of us," he says. "The next target might be you."

After Mitnick went to prison, a group of hackers called Hacking for Girliez (HFG) decided to declare their support of him in a very public way. In September 1998 they broke into the *New York Times* Web site and made alterations, including defacing the home page. Instead of the usual masthead, a black page with "HFG" in capital letters was in its place, with the name H4ACKING FOR GIRLI3Z beneath it. Other pages contained cryptically worded messages, many of which were threatening or sexually explicit. When *Times* officials learned what had happened, they took the site down in order to repair it. It was offline for days, which cost an estimated $1.5 million in lost revenue.

Quoted in Thomas C. Greene, "Chapter One: Kevin Mitnick's Story," Register, January 13, 2003.

Agency, which is charged with reducing threats to the United States and its allies from nuclear, biological, chemical, and other types of weapons. Once James had created a back door into the network, he was able to view thousands of confidential e-mails and capture employee user names and passwords.

When James hacked NASA's computers, he discovered serious security vulnerabilities, so he took the bold step of e-mailing system administrators to alert them. He told them exactly what the problems were and even how to fix them, but he knew they did not follow his advice because he continued to have access to the computers. They were aware of him, though. Even though James did not realize it, law enforcement officials were closely monitoring his activities. One day agents from the FBI and the Department of Defense unexpectedly showed up at his door. They confiscated all five of James's computers and left him with a stern warning. Then, several months later, he was arrested and convicted of his hacking crimes. He served six months in prison and, at the age of sixteen, was the youngest person to be incarcerated under the U.S. cybercrime law.

Today James is sometimes referred to as "Hacking's boy wonder," and he is listed as one of the ten most famous hackers of all time on numerous tech-related Web sites. He claims that he paid the price for his mistakes and has learned his lesson. Someday he may follow Kevin Mitnick's example and open his own computer security firm.

According to James, hackers like the sense of power they feel when they are able to crack the security of computers that belong to the government, the military, and large corporations. He explains: "It was a good feeling knowing I had access to the computers of the most powerful military in the world. I'm surprised my head didn't explode."[31] In an earlier interview, James said that even though many computers have sophisticated security systems in place, if hackers want to break in, they will break in, and nothing can stop them. "If there's a will, there's a way," he says, "and if a computer enthusiast such as myself was determined to get into anywhere, be it the Pentagon or Microsoft, it's been demonstrated that it's possible and they will do it. And there's next to nothing they can do about it, because there's people with skill out there, and they'll get what they want."[32]

Malicious Software

Of all the threats to computer systems throughout the world, malware is among the most dangerous. It can crash and even destroy entire computer systems, as well as enable cyber-criminals to steal personal information from unsuspecting users. Yet malware was not originally designed to cause destruction. The earliest versions were created by computer programmers, usually as experiments or pranks. For example, the first virus to strike personal computers was the Elk Cloner, which was created in 1982 by a ninth-grade hacker named Rich Skrenta. He wanted to play a practical joke on his friends, so he created a virus that would spread through floppy disks for the Apple II computer. Every fiftieth time someone booted an infected disk, the following Dr. Seuss–like verse from Skrenta appeared on the screen:

> Elk Cloner: The program with a personality
> It will get on all your disks
> It will infiltrate your chips
> Yes it's Cloner!
> It will stick to you like glue
> It will modify RAM too
> Send in the Cloner![33]

Nasty Code

Rather than causing lasting damage to computers, viruses such as the Elk Cloner were mostly annoyances that could be detected quickly and fixed in a day or two. But over the years malware has steadily grown more destructive and threatening. As an article in *Network Security Journal* explains: "Did you know that malicious-code writers now have a different set of rules of conduct? Gone are the days when they bragged about their successes—today it is a more driven approach towards making money rather than actually the thrill of hacking systems."[34]

Along with becoming more threatening, the volume of malware is multiplying at a rapid rate. According to the security firm Sophos, there were an estimated 9,450 malware threats in the spring of 2006. One year later, that number had climbed to nearly 24,000—a 150 percent increase. Symantec, another leading security firm, reports even more disturbing findings. In a September 2007 white paper, Symantec stated that during the first half of 2007, there were 212,101 new malicious code threats reported—which was a 185 percent increase over the second half of 2006. Dave DeWalt, president and CEO of security giant McAfee, adds his perspective on how fast these threats are growing:

> **By the Numbers**
>
> **200,000**
>
> **The number of new malicious code threats identified by McAfee in the first half of 2007.**

> We're overloaded with new malware being submitted in every shape and form. We're seeing 17,000 phishing attacks a month. It's so easy to do that we're seeing a tremendous rise in it. . . . It's nearly impossible to track them because they move so quickly and change their IP addresses so much. . . . When you see the number of attacks versus the number of people being caught, it's pretty miniscule.[35]

Drive-By Download

Whether malware is created for phishing schemes or other types of criminal acts, it is spread in different ways. The most common way is through e-mail attachments that contain malicious code; when unsuspecting users click on the attachments, their PCs become infected. Another method of spreading malware

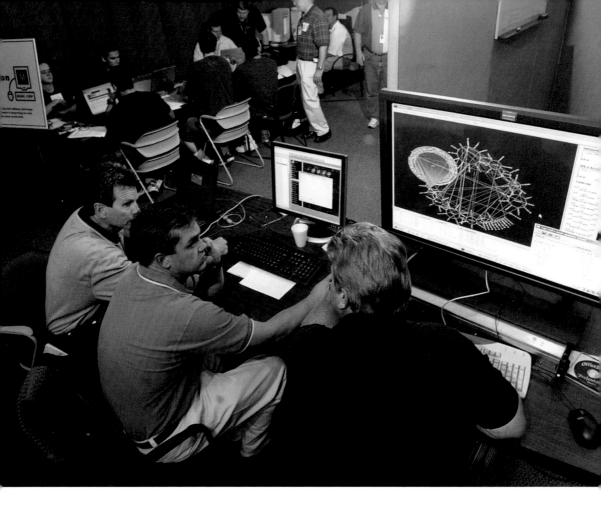

Employees at the virus protection company Symantec monitor computer networks during a barrage of malicious code attacks in 2004.

that is becoming increasingly prevalent is infected Web sites. According to Sophos technology consultant Graham Cluley, an average of eight thousand new URLs containing malware were discovered each week during April 2007. During that month, technology professionals at Google examined 4.5 million Web sites and found that one out of every ten pages was infected with malicious code. In a follow-up report, Google stated that the attackers' goal was to identify Web applications that were older and more vulnerable because they were not kept up to date with security patches. Small pieces of malicious code were inserted within the sites' HTML programming code, causing them to become infected with malware. Thus, unsuspecting users who visited these infected sites were at risk for having malicious code automatically installed on their own machines, which is known as a drive-by download.

In November 2007 a number of MySpace sites belonging to popular musicians, including singer Alicia Keys, were infected by malicious software. When users tried to access one of the hacked sites, the malware attempted to install itself on their computers. If that failed, users were asked to install a program (known as a codec) that would allow them to view a streaming video on the page. If they clicked the link that was given, instead of being able to view the video, another announcement popped up asking them to install a different kind of software known as an ActiveX control, which automatically downloaded malicious software. This allowed hackers to hijack their computers and take control of them.

"Everyone Should Be on Their Guard"

The type of malware that infected Alicia Keys's Web site was a Trojan horse, which is a computer program that pretends to be legitimate, but has malicious code (known as a payload) secretly concealed inside it. In addition to Web sites, Trojan horses are often distributed through bogus e-mails, fake online greeting cards, screensavers, or fake anti-spyware programs. In order for Trojan horses to spread, users must invite them in, such as by clicking into infected Web sites or opening e-mail attachments.

During a June 2007 phishing attack, hackers sent out e-mails that pretended to be from Microsoft. The e-mails looked official because they displayed the Microsoft logo and were personally addressed with people's names and companies. They warned recipients that a security problem had been discovered in a Microsoft e-mail program and encouraged them to download a patch that would fix the problem and protect them from being attacked by hackers. Those who clicked on the link, however, were not taken to Microsoft's Web site as promised. Instead, they ended up on a malicious site that hosted a Trojan horse. Graham Cluley, Sophos senior technology consultant, explains: "By using people's real names, the

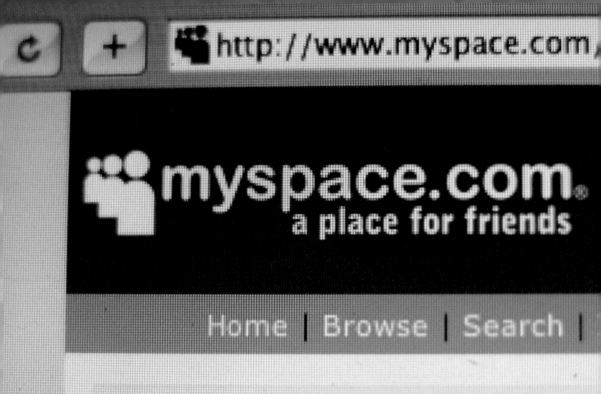

Hackers often attempt to gain entry into popular sites like MySpace. They infect the site with malicious software.

Microsoft logo, and legitimate-sounding wording, the hackers are attempting to fool more people into stepping blindly into their bear-trap. Users need to be on their guard against this kind of confidence trick or they risk handing over control of their PC to hackers with criminal intentions."[36]

In October 2005 a Trojan horse was found circulating on some popular video game sites. Users were deceived by it because it was designed to look like a patch for the Sony PlayStation Portable (PSP) game device. When they installed it, thinking they would download the patch, the message, "Your PSP 2.0 is hacked, please reboot" popped up on their console screen. Restarting it proved to be impossible, however, because the Trojan had deleted four critical system files and rendered the PSP useless. Symantec security official Richard Archdeacon explains how serious the damage was: "The device basically becomes a brick. You might as well use it to build a house."[37]

One of the most common reasons that malicious hackers create Trojan horses is to steal personal information. In February 2007 the FBI arrested a Washington man named Richard Honour for creating and distributing a Trojan horse that was designed to steal user names and passwords. The malware affected users who frequented DarkMyst, an online chat room that is popular with computer game fans. Honour sent messages that claimed to contain links to online movies—but when users clicked on the links, their computers were infected with a Trojan horse. It allowed Honour to spy on them, as well as gain access to bank and credit card numbers and commit identity theft. Says Cluley:

> Criminals like Richard Honour lure the unwary by disguising their Trojan horses as seemingly harmless links to movie files. The rise of the Trojan has been one of the key developments in cybercrime in recent years, as hackers increasingly use them to steal information and money from unsuspecting internet users. Everyone should be on their guard against this type of attack.[38]

Viruses and Bombs

Like Trojan horses, computer viruses require user interaction before they can cause infection. This often happens when users click on an e-mail attachment, download an infected file from the Internet, or visit an infected Web site. A virus passes from one computer to another in the same way as a real-life biological virus passes from person to person, as tech writer Kim Zetter explains: "Computer viruses are the 'common cold' of modern technology. They can spread swiftly across open networks such

By the Numbers

$1,000 TO $5,000

The cost range advertised in underground hacking forums for a Trojan horse that is designed to transfer funds between online accounts.

45

How a Spearphishing Attack Works

Many hackers are skilled programmers, and those who are motivated to cause malicious acts have the skill to fool unsuspecting computer users with targeted spearphishing attacks.

1 First the Trojan horse or worm is developed, either by repackaging existing malware or creating a new version from scratch.

2 Once the malware is created, the hacker breaks into target companies' Web sites to extract names and e-mail addresses of authority figures and employees and also to find out what antivirus software the company uses.

3 The hacker downloads the latest version of that antivirus software to make sure the new Trojan horse can break through it.

4 A meticulously crafted spearphishing e-mail is created using the information previously gathered, and the Trojan horse is embedded in the e-mail.

5 The e-mail, which appears to be from an authority figure in the company or other trusted source, is sent to a targeted list of employees.

6 If an employee opens the attachment, the Trojan horse executes in the background.

7 Once the victim's computer has been infected, the hacker can take control of it and steal confidential information.

as the Internet, causing billions of dollars worth of damage in a short amount of time."[39] Unlike Trojan horses, though, viruses spread by self-replicating, or making copy after copy of themselves.

Viruses may harm computers by damaging or corrupting programs; deleting files; executing random text, audio, and video messages; depleting memory; slowing down operations; or completely reformatting hard disks, which causes all data to be erased. One of the most dangerous and destructive viruses of all time was known as CIH, which was unleashed from Taiwan in April 1999. The virus infected older versions of the Microsoft Windows operating system, including Windows 95, 98, and ME. Once it had been activated, it overwrote data on computer hard drives, making the systems inoperable. CIH infections were widespread, affecting hundreds of thousands of computers in Turkey, Korea, and the United States.

Once users open a file or application that has been infected by a virus, the malicious code burrows into a file in their computer system. There it waits until it is time to deliver the payload that the creator programmed into it. Viruses that have delayed payloads are sometimes referred to as bombs. For instance, time bombs are set to perform malicious acts on a specific date or time, while logic bombs occur when a computer use takes a particular action that triggers it. A logic bomb might be triggered at a specified time on a computer's internal clock, or whenever certain files or programs are altered or deleted.

In May 2006 a former government contractor created a logic bomb that could have resulted in disaster. Richard Sylvestra programmed malicious software codes into five computers that track U.S. Navy submarines at a site in Naples, Italy. After Sylvestra released the logic bomb, he fled the country and was later caught and sentenced to a year in prison. Only three of the five computers he sabotaged were shut down—but if he had succeeded in harming all of them, the entire network would have been disabled. According to Navy officials, that could have led to catastrophe. Submarines would not have been able to detect hazards, including other submarines, and could easily have crashed into each other.

Insidious Worms

Like viruses, worms also replicate themselves as they travel through network connections, looking for vulnerable computers with security holes. Worms often carry harmful payloads and have the ability to propagate very, very quickly. On July 19, 2001, for instance, the Code Red worm replicated itself more than 350,000 times in just fourteen hours.

One important difference between worms and viruses is that users do not have to invite a worm into a computer. Although worms are sometimes spread through e-mail attachments, they are often unleashed directly on the Internet by their creators. Once a worm has been released, it begins slithering through the Net on its own, scanning connected computers to find those that have not been security patched, and leaving destruction in its wake. In January 2003 the Slammer worm infected the private computer network of the Davis-Besse nuclear power station in Oak Harbor, Ohio. The worm infestation caused the computer system to crash, which led to the plant's safety monitoring systems being disabled for nearly five hours.

During the summer of 2005, the Zotob worm, created by Farid Essebar of Morocco and Atilla Ekici of Turkey, swept across the Internet and infected thousands of computers. The worm caused servers to reboot repeatedly, which created serious business disruptions for the CNN and ABC networks, the Canadian bank CIBC, and the *Financial Times* and the *New York Times* newspapers. Zotob also created chaos for thirteen of DaimlerChrysler's automobile manufacturing plants in Michigan, Illinois, Indiana, Ohio, Delaware, and Wisconsin. The worm knocked computer systems offline for close to an hour. This brought assembly operations to a halt and left fifty thousand assembly line employees unable to work until the infected systems were cleaned and patched.

An even more destructive computer worm known as Sasser was unleashed by a German teenager named Sven Jaschan in April 2004. The worm spread quickly, crippling computer systems throughout the world. Sasser's infestation was responsible for shutting down British Airways flight check-ins at London's Heathrow Airport, causing delays to twenty-one of the airline's flights and disrupting the schedules of thousands of travelers.

The worm also created problems for Air Canada, American Express, the investment bank Goldman Sachs, Sampo Bank in Finland, and several schools, including the University of California, Irvine and University of Massachusetts at Amherst. It hit all nineteen of Great Britain's Coast Guard control centers, causing computers to crash. Computers in half of Taiwan's post offices were infected, as were government agencies in Hong Kong and computers at a hospital in Lund, Sweden. Several oil platforms in the Gulf of Mexico were out of commission for several days. Problems with computers at the Australian Railcorp caused trains to stop running because it was impossible for drivers to talk to signalmen.

After the Slammer worm was unleashed, safety monitoring systems were shut down for five hours at the Davis-Besse nuclear plant in Ohio.

The Sasser worm infected millions of computers worldwide. It likely caused billions of dollars in damages, although the exact amount may never be known, as security expert Dave Rand explains: "There have been huge estimates as to the costs related to Sasser but the real damage was in the clean up. It took out email and it took out infrastructure but the actual damage is impossible to quantify—but it was huge."[40] Jaschan pled guilty to all the charges against him, including computer sabotage, and could have faced five years in prison for his crime. But because he was only seventeen years old when he was arrested, he was tried as a juvenile and sentenced to twenty-one months' probation and thirty hours of community service.

"They Trade Bot Nets Like Candy"

Worms such as Sasser, as well as viruses and Trojan horses, have caused immense damage to computer systems. But the newest versions of malware are becoming far more sophisticated than ever before—as well as more dangerous. Cybercriminals are hijacking scores of computers, turning them into "zombies," or robotlike machines that the hackers control remotely. Technical writer Brian Krebs explains: "Hacked, remote-controlled home computers, known as robots or 'bots,' and large groups of robot networks . . . called 'botnets' are the souped-up cyber engines driving nearly all criminal commerce on the Internet."[41] The hackers create malware that is designed to scour the Internet, looking for vulnerable computers that can be infected. According to security experts, this usually happens without users ever knowing that their computers have been compromised. The zombie computers can then be programmed to scan the Internet for more vulnerable machines to infect, further expanding a hacker's zombie fleet. According to a September 2007 report by Arbor Networks researchers, it is likely that tens of millions of computers worldwide are infected with botnet programs.

Bot herders, or bot masters, are hackers who create and run the botnets, and they often have thousands of machines under their control. They are part of a secretive computer gang that the FBI calls the Botmaster Underground, and they meet in online forums to exchange ideas and trade malware and bots. Nicholas Albright, the founder of the security group ShadowServer, says that this is a common practice among young hackers, as he explains: "I see high school kids doing it all the time. They trade bot nets like candy."[42] Bot herders use their networks of zombie computers to send out millions of spam e-mail messages and pop-up ads that promote everything from prescription medications to Rolex watches. In many cases, they are paid to do the spamming by advertising companies such as Gamma-Cash and TopConverting.

Botnets are also used to spread a type of malicious code known as spyware (or adware), which is designed to capture personal information from users' computers. Although much spyware is harmless, some is designed to be used for malicious purposes. During the summer of 2007, botnets were used to break into the job recruitment Web site Monster.com on at least two occasions, which resulted in the theft of millions of job seekers' confidential data. The stolen information was used by hackers to craft personalized phishing e-mails that were sent to job seekers. If the recipients fell for the trick, spyware or other malicious software was secretly installed on their computers. After the breach, Monster.com president Sal Iannuzzi admitted that the site may never be completely safe: "I want to be clear and I want to be frank: there is no guaranteed fix. I wish I could say there will be absolutely no way that the Monster site can be compromised. I cannot ever make that promise, and no [Internet] company can."[43]

Some criminal hackers use botnets to demand large amounts of money from businesses. According to the Internet security experts, the hackers usually start by launching a small, short attack to scare the target business and get its attention.

The Morris Worm

In November 1988, a Cornell University graduate student named Robert Tappan Morris created the very first Internet worm. As soon as he unleashed it, the worm began racing through the Internet, multiplying and infecting computer systems at a much faster rate than Morris had anticipated. Soon computers throughout the country were crashing or becoming completely unresponsive to commands, including machines at NASA, military agencies, several universities, and medical research facilities. Realizing that the worm was out of control, Morris worked with a friend to try to stop it. They sent anonymous messages to system administrators to explain how to kill the worm and patch vulnerable systems, but few received the e-mail because they had been forced to disconnect from the Internet. Eventually, however, the worm was stopped, but by that time the damages it had caused were estimated at $15 million.

Morris was arrested, and although he claimed that he had never intended to cause harm or damage, he was convicted in 1990 of violating the Computer Fraud and Abuse Act (Title 18). He was fined and sentenced to three years' probation and four hundred hours of community service. He was also expelled from Cornell.

Former Cornell student Robert T. Morris, shown here, created the Internet's first worm. Morris said he never meant any harm.

Soon afterward, an extortion-type letter is sent to the business requesting protection money, or a request for payment that will ensure there will be no further attacks. "This is almost identical to a Mafia protection racket," says Dave Matthews, site administrator of the online publication "Las Vegas Advisor." "It's the same as going into the store and saying 'pay me and I'll guarantee your store won't burn down for a year.' It's just more high tech."[44] If businesses refuse to pay, the botnets are programmed to launch DDoS attacks. This bombards the companies' Web sites with meaningless data and causes their computer systems to crash, which can cost thousands of dollars in lost revenue. Either way, the results can be disastrous.

The Rise and Fall of the Zombie King

One of the most notorious bot herders is a California man named Jeanson James Ancheta, who once bragged that hacking into PCs connected to the Internet was "easy, like slicing cheese."[45] He was quite confident that he was unstoppable—but he was eventually caught and sent to prison for his crimes.

Known as the Zombie King, Ancheta controlled a massive bot network during 2004 and 2005 that included more than four hundred thousand computers. Among those were machines that belonged to the Defense Information Systems Agency of the Department of Defense in Arlington, Virginia, and the Weapons Division of the U.S. Naval Air Warfare Center in China Lake, California. According to U.S. Department of Justice documents, Ancheta started by developing a Trojan horse program called rxbot, which allowed him to create botnets that he used to distribute spam and spyware for advertising service companies. He earned hefty commissions for his spamming efforts. He also made money by renting access to his botnets to other hackers, usually in increments of ten thousand computers at a time, so they could distribute spam or launch DDoS attacks. Ancheta advertised the botnets in a private Internet chat area under the heading "#botz4sale." Included in his rental price was a detailed set of guidelines, including information about how many zombies would be needed to crash corporate Web sites of various sizes.

Ancheta's online advertising eventually proved to be his downfall. The FBI, which was already investigating fast-growing zombie networks and knew they were a major threat, noticed his online ad and price list. Agents from Los Angeles started posing undercover in chat rooms, where they talked to Ancheta and asked him to help them launch DDoS attacks. The FBI explains his reaction: "After bragging to us about making $1,000 in just two weeks, Ancheta sold us 2,000 bots, promising they'd be 'enough to drop a site.' We seized Ancheta's computer in December 2004 and eventually put him out of business for good in May 2005 when we disabled the servers he was using."[46] The FBI continued to gather evidence and arrested Ancheta in November 2005. He was indicted for seventeen counts of conspiracy and computer crime, including violation of the U.S.

Bot herder Jeanson James Ancheta, alias the Zombie King, hacked his way into vital Department of Defense computers, shown here.

Computer Fraud Abuse Act and antispam laws. The following May he was sentenced to nearly five years in federal prison, followed by three years of supervised release.

James Aquilina, the assistant U.S. attorney who prosecuted Ancheta on behalf of the federal government, said the sentence was the longest one ever handed down for a case involving the spread of computer viruses. Aquilina hopes that the stiff punishment sends a strong message to other bot masters and malicious young hackers, as he explains: "A lot of people thought [Ancheta] would simply get a slap on the wrist and never get any real jail time. My hope is that this sentence will deter others from using botnets to commit crimes, especially the youthful ones who commit these crimes and think they're immune from prosecution, that they'll never get caught."[47] The Zombie King learned the hard way that if a criminal hacker does get caught, there is a tough price to pay.

CHAPTER 4

Cyberterrorism

Today the word *terrorism* is widely understood by people throughout the world. It involves the unlawful use, or threatened use, of force or violence in order to accomplish goals that are often political or religious in nature. Cyberterrorism, which is not so well known, refers to the merging of cyberspace (the Internet) and terrorist acts. The term is sometimes confused with malicious hacking, but the two are not the same. Cyberterrorism is much more serious—and far more potentially destructive and dangerous. Dr. Dorothy Denning, a security expert and professor at the Naval Postgraduate School in Monterey, California, offers the following definition:

> Cyberterrorism . . . refers to unlawful attacks and threats of attacks against computers, networks and the information stored therein when done to intimidate or coerce a government or its people in furtherance of political or social objectives. Further, to qualify as cyberterrorism, an attack should result in violence against persons or property, or at least cause enough harm to generate fear. Attacks that lead to death or bodily injury, explosions, or severe economic loss would be examples. . . . Attacks that disrupt nonessential services or that are mainly a costly nuisance would not.[48]

How Likely Is Cyberterrorism?

As frightening as the idea of cyberterrorism is, the threat is based on the possibility of what *could* happen, rather than what *has* happened. Even with all the cybercrimes that have been committed by hackers, none has ever been classified as an act of cyberterrorism. Some people are convinced that the risks are blown out of proportion, especially by the media. They point out that fears of cyberterrorism are based solely on hypothetical incidents, and there is no evidence to show that terrorists could or would actually launch a cyberattack. In his article "The Myth of Cyberterrorism," journalist Joshua Green says that there is no compelling evidence that al Qaeda or any other terrorist organization has ever used computers for destructive activity. He insists that cyberterrorism threats are exaggerated

By the Numbers

7,000 +

The number of terrorist Web sites that cyber security experts believe are online.

and largely based on public ignorance, and says that the billions of dollars in damage caused to the American economy each year by computer hackers is a much more serious threat. "What's more," he writes, "outside of a Tom Clancy novel, computer security specialists believe it is virtually impossible to use the Internet to inflict death on a large scale, and many scoff at the notion that terrorists would bother trying."[49]

Dorothy Denning is another person who downplays the risk of cyberterrorism. She maintains that there are no terrorist plans to conduct cyberattacks, nor do terrorist groups have the capability of launching such attacks. She says that terrorist organizations are known to favor violent incidents that capture mass publicity and bring worldwide attention to their causes. As she explains, "[Terrorists] haven't pursued this kind of attack because it's not bloody. Terrorism is built around physical attacks with bombs."[50] Denning adds that the threat of cyberterrorism is nowhere near as serious as the threat of weapons of mass destruction or violent acts such as car bombs or suicide bombers.

According to Dan Verton, even though cyberterrorism does not necessarily involve traditional acts of violence, it would be an attractive weapon for terrorists because it could cause disastrous damage to the American economy. Banks and other financial institutions, major corporations, and the

An expert monitors a transportation control center. Many worry that such infrastructures are vulnerable to attack by cyberterrorists.

New York Stock Exchange all conduct business online. If a cyberattack were serious enough, there could be a ripple effect; financial transactions worldwide would be disrupted or halted, businesses could suffer billions of dollars in losses, and stock prices would begin to tumble. This would erode public confidence and lead to widespread fear and uncertainty—which is a primary goal of terrorism. As Verton explains:

> Most people have a hard time accepting the notion of terrorism on the Internet—a legitimate argument, since nobody has or will ever be gunned down in a digital hail of ones and zeros shooting out of a computer, traveling across the Internet, and ripping through the side of a bus on its way to a religious celebration. But therein lies the fundamental misinterpretation that most people have about cyber-terrorism. In cyber-terrorism, the economy of the enemy nation is the target, and death and destruction are considered a welcome blend

of collateral damage if the attackers can arrange it. In cyber-terrorism, the goal is to cut the digital arteries of the economy and the companies that make up the economy, leaving them to bleed money and resources into the streets.[51]

Those who agree with Verton believe that just because no cyberterrorist attacks have happened yet, it does not change the fact that they could happen at any time. In a February 2002 statement, Senator Chuck Schumer warned about the dangers of cyberterrorism, particularly in New York. Because New York is America's largest metropolitan area and is the epicenter of commerce, technology, and transportation, Schumer cautioned that it is the country's most obvious—and vulnerable—target. Schumer said:

> The odds and danger of a cyber attack grow by the day and we're doing virtually nothing about it. We're not just talking about losing email for a few hours. Terrorists like Hamas or Al Qaeda could gain access to our power plants, . . . our utilities, and our banking systems, which translates into rolling blackouts, dead phone lines, and wiped out bank accounts. Some experts have described us as being vulnerable to a digital Pearl Harbor. Frankly, I fear we're on the verge of a digital Armageddon.[52]

Built-In Protection

One reason there is such controversy about the risk of cyber-terrorism is because there are many myths associated with it. For instance, in the 1983 movie *War Games*, a teenage computer genius manages to hack into the Pentagon's defense system. By simulating nuclear weapon deployment, the young man comes close to starting World War III. Of course, *War Games* was just a movie, and purely a work of fiction.

A Road Map for Cyberterrorists

Sean Gorman, a graduate student from George Mason University, wrote his PhD dissertation on America's critical infrastructure—or more specifically, how vulnerable it is to terrorist attacks. Gorman mapped every business and industrial sector in the country, as well as the fiber-optic network that connects them. A July 2003 article in the *Washington Post* describes how meticulous his work was: "He can click on a bank in Manhattan and see who has communication lines running into it and where. He can zoom in on Baltimore and find the choke point for trucking warehouses. He can drill into a cable trench between Kansas and Colorado and determine how to create the most havoc with a hedge clipper. Using mathematical formulas, he probes for critical links, trying to answer the question: 'If I were Osama bin Laden, where would I want to attack?'"

When government officials learned about the document, they were alarmed, saying that if it were to fall into terrorists' hands, it could serve as a step-by-step guide for destroying the country's critical infrastructures. Richard Clarke, the former White House cyberterrorism chief, said that once the dissertation had been turned in and Gorman got his grade, it should be burned. "The fiber-optic network is our country's nervous system," he said. "You don't want to give terrorists a road map to blow that up." Surprisingly enough, however, Gorman did not access any classified information to write the document. Every single bit of information he included was freely available to the public on the Internet.

Sean Gorman, shown here, caught the attention of the U.S. Homeland Security department after he mapped the country's fiber-optic network.

Quoted in Laura Blumenfeld, "Dissertation Could Be Security Threat," Washington Post, July 8, 2003. www.washingtonpost.com/ac2/ wp-dyn/A23689-2003Jul7?language=printer.

But some people have the perception that the movie could become reality because nuclear weapons may be triggered from remote locations. That is not true, however. Nuclear weapons and other sensitive U.S. Department of Defense systems are "air-gapped," which means they are not connected to the Internet and are not accessible to hackers. The same is true with other key government systems, as John Gilligan of the Air Force explains: "Terrorists could not gain control of our spacecraft, nuclear weapons, or any other type of high-consequence asset."[53] In addition to military agencies' systems being air-gapped, so are the computer networks of the FBI and the CIA.

Another fear is that cyberterrorists could gain control of the Federal Aviation Administration's (FAA) air traffic control system and shut it down, which would obviously lead to massive catastrophe. But like many other government computer systems, the FAA's air traffic control system is air-gapped. As a result, it would likely be impossible for terrorists to break into the system and hijack airplanes from remote locations.

The Power Grid

Even though cyberterrorists cannot use the Internet to seize control of American airplanes, spacecraft, or weapons, there is a different sort of risk that concerns many security experts. They say that if terrorists were to launch a cyberattack, a likely target would be America's critical infrastructures. These are the complex, interdependent systems, networks, and assets that serve large populations throughout the country. Often referred to as the power grid, critical infrastructures are divided into separate sectors. They include electrical power generation; oil and gas refineries; nuclear reactors, materials, and waste;

By the Numbers

$700 BILLION

The estimated loss to the United States economy if a cyberterrorist attack caused a third of the country to lose power for three months.

hydroelectric facilities and dams; manufacturing; drinking water and wastewater treatment systems; telecommunications; emergency services; energy, food, and agriculture; and primary data storage and processing facilities, stock exchanges, and major financial centers, among others. These infrastructures are essential for modern society and the economy to function properly. According to the Critical Infrastructure Protection Program at George Mason University School of Law, critical infrastructures "drive all of the necessary functions upon which society depends, yet, for the most part, completely ignores. . . . [These are] basic services that we continually rely on day after day, services that enable us to heat or cool our homes, talk to one another over the telephone, travel to work, and even have clean water to drink."[54]

Employees at a systems operation center observe power grids. An attack on such a critical infrastructure could be devastating.

If the country's power grid were seriously disabled or disrupted, the consequences could be disastrous, including severe economic losses and loss of life—and according to some gov-

ernment officials and security experts, that is a very real possibility. Israeli terrorism expert Gabriel Weimann says that if terrorists were able to gain access to these infrastructures and alter or destroy them, it would threaten regional and possibly national security. "Just as the events of 9/11 caught the world by surprise," he writes, "so could a major cyberassault. The threat of cyberterrorism may be exaggerated and manipulated, but we can neither deny it nor dare to ignore it."[55]

In a December 2003 statement on critical infrastructure protection, President George W. Bush spoke about the risks of cyberterrorism. He said that it was a very real threat that needed to be taken seriously because terrorists want to do whatever they can

> to threaten national security, cause mass casualties, weaken our economy, and damage public morale and confidence. . . . Critical infrastructure and key resources provide the essential services that underpin American society. The Nation possesses numerous key resources, whose exploitation or destruction by terrorists could cause catastrophic health effects or mass casualties comparable to those from the use of a weapon of mass destruction, or could profoundly affect our national prestige and morale.[56]

Bush went on to say that he considers it a national priority to protect the United States' critical infrastructures from terrorist attacks.

The Vulnerability of SCADA

The sole reason that cyberterrorism is a threat to infrastructures is because the numerous industries that comprise it are connected to the Internet. Computerized process control systems, known as Supervisory Control and Data Acquisition (SCADA), are used by most industries. Major electrical utilities and telecommunications companies rely on SCADA systems for their day-to-day operations, as do water treatment plants, chemical factories, environmental control operations, oil and gas refineries, and manufacturing firms. Dan Verton writes:

> All of the things we take for granted in our everyday lives, such as electricity, telephone and Internet service, the 911 emergency system, air traffic control systems, banks and ATM machines, credit card systems . . . waterways and railroads, hospitals and critical life-saving medical equipment . . . and a host of other so-called "critical infrastructures," rely on computers and computer networks for their management and continued operation.[57]

SCADA systems digitize and automate tasks that were once handled by human workers, such as opening and closing valves in circuit breakers, monitoring temperatures and pressures in reactors, gauging fuel levels, controlling alarms, and managing assembly lines.

SCADA technology has been around since the 1960s. Originally it had nothing to do with the Internet because the Internet did not yet exist. SCADA systems were proprietary networks, mostly owned by private enterprises rather than government agencies. Even though they were developed for maximum efficiency rather than security, they were considered secure because they were not accessible through any sort of global connection.

In recent years, however, more and more companies have begun merging their SCADA operation control systems with their Internet-connected corporate networks. This convergence allows industries to realize greater efficiencies, lower costs, and higher profitability. Engineers and plant managers can now control operations from their desktop computers or from remote access through wireless connections or dial-up modems, which is a great convenience for them. But along with the advantages of interconnectivity there is increased risk.

Because SCADA systems are now connected to the Internet, cyberterrorists could conceivably access the nation's critical infrastructures and wreak havoc on them. Gail Thackery, Arizona's assistant attorney, discusses the reality of this threat: "Are we vulnerable? Absolutely. We have the massive bowl of spaghetti between the Internet, phone lines, and extranets, and no one can map it. We have miles and miles and miles of wire and none of it is secure. And we have all those windows and doors that are open, and they are still open."[58]

According to security expert Rich Mogull, many SCADA controllers and servers now run on the Microsoft Windows operating system, which has repeatedly been the target of malicious hacking attacks. Also, SCADA systems, many of which are old, were not designed to be used with security devices such as firewalls and intrusion detection systems, and they cannot be patched. This makes the systems especially vulnerable to destructive worms, computer viruses, and other

A power grid pinpointing various power facilities is an open target and is especially vulnerable to cyberterrorism.

malicious software. Mogull adds that there have been actual attacks on such systems. During the Slammer worm infestation, for instance, a safety system at a nuclear power plant crashed, and the Blaster worm contributed to a power outage in the Northeast. Mogull also cites an occasion when he was attending a private meeting in a foreign country and learned that on multiple occasions, hackers had gained access to the local train control system and were able to control the trains. Even though these were not acts of cyberterrorism, they were examples of what sort of destruction could occur in the event of an actual cyberterrorist attack.

An "Open Target"

Along with infrastructure vulnerabilities, another factor that concerns many security experts and government officials is that terrorist presence on the Internet is skyrocketing. Security specialist Hsinchun Chen says that since the September 11, 2001, attacks on America, the number of terrorist groups online "has multiplied tenfold. Around the year 2000, there were 70 to 80 core terrorist sites online; now there are at least 7000 to 8000. . . . [The Internet] is arguably the most powerful tool for spreading extremist violence around the world."[59]

Also, intelligence officials know that terrorists collect information on American infrastructures. Raids in Afghanistan during 2002 uncovered that al Qaeda members had been closely scrutinizing American Web sites that contained information about SCADA networks. Their laptop computers had structural and engineering software, electronic models of dams, and information about water systems, nuclear power plants, and major stadiums in the United States and Europe. In the years since then, research has shown that al Qaeda and other terrorist groups have become more technologically sophisticated than ever before. They are well aware of American computer security weaknesses because there has been much worldwide publicity about it—which means they

are also aware that the U.S. economy could be greatly harmed by cyberterrorism. This became apparent in December 2001, when Osama bin Laden appeared in a videotape, urging the destruction of the U.S. economy. "This economic hemorrhaging continues until today, but requires more blows," he said. "And the youth should try to find the joints of the American economy and hit the enemy in these joints, with God's permission."[60]

In a February 2004 testimony before the U.S. Senate Committee on the Judiciary, FBI Cyber Division Deputy Assistant Director Keith Lourdeau confirmed that terrorist groups are continuously becoming more technically competent; as they become more familiar with computers, they are likely to pursue acts of cyberterrorism. He said that the FBI

Videotape shows an al Qaeda operative in Afghanistan using sophisticated computer communications. Osama bin Laden has urged attacks on the U.S. economy.

considers cyberterrorism to be a very real threat to the United States, and the threat is expanding rapidly. "Terrorist groups have shown a clear interest in developing basic hacking tools and the FBI predicts that terrorist groups will either develop or hire hackers, particularly for the purpose of complementing large physical attacks with cyber attacks. . . . [I]n the future cyberterrorism may become a viable option to traditional physical acts of violence."[61]

In April 2003 a security expert identified only as a "master hacker" was interviewed by PBS. He stated that not only are American infrastructures highly vulnerable, the United States is likely more vulnerable than any other country. That, he says, is because information technology and communications technology are at the very root of America's livelihood. He says that the United States is an "open target" and makes it clear that cyberterrorism is a real threat that needs to be taken seriously and addressed before disaster happens. "Just as Sept. 11 proved that America is no longer an island, that the capabilities inherent in the way America works can be turned against it—crashing our own jets into our own skyscrapers—once the bad guys, whoever they may be, figure out that the U.S. infrastructure really is vulnerable, really is as porous as it truly is, then the attacks won't stop."[62]

The Aurora Experiment

Because cyberterrorism poses such a risk to critical infrastructures, security professionals often stage experimental operations to assess potential damage. One such experiment, dubbed Aurora, was conducted in March 2007 on a power generator at the U.S. Department of Energy's laboratory in Idaho. The experiment served as a mock cyberattack, whereby researchers hacked into a replica of a power plant's control system and changed the operating cycle of the generator. After a short time the generator self-destructed—it shuddered and shook violently, and then went up in a plume of black smoke.

A Taste of Cyberterrorism

The vulnerability of critical infrastructures is an issue of concern for security professionals, industry executives, and government officials. Although hackers have targeted critical infrastructures in the past, there has never been an attack that proved to be cyberterrorism. But in early 2000 a frightening incident in Australia gave people a glimpse of the damage that cyberterrorists might be able to cause.

An Australian man named Vitek Boden had been turned down for a job with the Maroochy Shire Council in Queensland. He set up his car as a remote command center, and, using a laptop computer fitted with a radio transmitter, he hacked into the system and altered pump station operations at Pacific Paradise. His actions caused more than 264,000 gallons (1 million L) of raw, smelly sewage to gush into waterways, parks, and the grounds of a Hyatt Regency hotel. The disastrous sewage spill turned creeks black, contaminating water, killing marine life, and leaving a horrible stench in its wake. Officials found that it was an act of revenge by a disgruntled man, rather than an act of cyberterrorism—but it definitely got their attention. According to security expert Dorothy Denning, Boden's malicious act was the most serious attack that had ever been reported against a critical infrastructure.

The Aurora experiment was alarming to people connected with it because they say the same sort of attack could potentially be launched against huge generators that produce electrical power throughout America. They believe that it was a wake-up call because of what could potentially happen on a larger scale—simultaneous, coordinated cyberattacks on key electrical facilities that could cause widespread damage by knocking out power to large geographic areas for months at a time. According to Scott Borg, who is the director and chief economist with the U.S. Cyber Consequences Unit, if a third of the country lost power for three months, the economic cost could top $700 billion. "It's equivalent to 40 to 50 large hurricanes striking all at once," he says. "It's greater economic damage than any modern economy ever suffered."[63]

Cyberterrorism Tomorrow

Many security experts say that the greatest potential damage from cyberterrorism would result from a multipronged attack, also known as swarming. For example, if terrorists detonated bombs at the same time they disrupted rescue efforts by disabling the 911 emergency telephone system, it could result in widespread disaster and send the entire country into a state of panic. As Todd Datz explains: "Think 9/11, but magnify the chaos by adding an electronic knockout of regional or national communication and power systems."[64]

Even though there is vast disagreement about whether cyberterrorism is a real-world threat or nothing more than hyperbole and media hype, it is definitely a topic that is widely discussed among security experts, technology professionals, corporate executives, and government officials. According to Richard Clarke, former White House counterterrorism adviser and national security adviser, it is time for people to stop ignoring the risk of cyberterrorism and realize that it is a serious threat. Says Clarke:

> In World War II countries flew heavy bombers over the enemy's cities to blow up communication nodes and electrical power stations. In the next war that effort may not be necessary. Electrical power grids and telecommunication grids are computer-controlled and linked over fairly open-access communication systems. It is now possible to hack one's way into such systems,

take control of the controlling computer systems, and disable electrical power grids and telephones as surely as if they had been destroyed.[65]

Whether Clarke's dismal prediction is correct or overblown, no one can say for sure. But those who agree with him believe that it is much smarter to err on the side of caution and plan for such disasters than to risk catastrophe by pretending that the threat of cyberterrorism does not exist.

CHAPTER 5

Can Computer Hackers Be Stopped?

As hackers become more sophisticated and ruthless, the destruction they cause to computer systems grows more threatening every day. Law enforcement officials from the FBI, CIA, Department of Homeland Security, and other government agencies, as well as private security professionals, are constantly working on ways to stop these criminals from performing their illegal and dangerous acts. Yet they know what a daunting task that is. In the November 2007 *Virtual Criminology Report*, McAfee president Dave DeWalt writes that cybercrime is a major problem that continues to grow at an alarming rate:

> The experts agree that cybercrime has evolved significantly in complexity and scope. . . . The unfortunate reality is that no one is immune from this malicious industry's reach—individuals, businesses, even governments. As the world has flattened, we've seen a significant amount of emerging threats from increasingly sophisticated groups attacking organizations around the world. And it's only going to get worse.[66]

"A Cat and Mouse Game"

A big reason why cybercrime is flourishing throughout the world is that hackers are cunning and know how to cover their tracks. They pride themselves on being able to break through security systems and outsmart people who are trying to catch them. Jack Blaisdale (not his real name) is a former police officer who worked undercover for years to catch computer hackers and other cyber criminals. He explains the challenges for law enforcement:

> It's a cat and mouse game—every advance on one side is matched by one on the other. Like all criminals, hackers constantly look for new "ins" and score status among their fellow hackers when they crack through code that's been deemed unbreakable. For every one that's caught and put behind bars, there are hundreds more that go undetected. It's a tough problem to solve—and it's not getting any easier.[67]

Blaisdale adds that in an alarming number of cases, cyber-crimes are not the result of hacking at all; rather, they happen because of carelessness on the part of computer users. He says that far too many people do not take appropriate measures to protect themselves against attacks. Many use simple passwords that are easy to remember, rather than choosing passwords that would be difficult for hackers to guess. Also, users are often tricked by savvy hackers into giving up passwords and other confidential data, as Blaisdale explains: "Little known fact: The huge majority of so-called 'hacks' are nothing more than social engineering. Using a phone or e-mail, the hacker simply talks his way into the network by convincing some-one to give up a password, login information, or other critical information—therefore, educating users to not fall for such tricks would block a LOT of 'hacks.'"[68]

Preventive Education

The effectiveness of such social engineer-ing tactics became apparent in March 2005, when the U.S. Treasury Department performed a security test with employees of the Internal Revenue Service (IRS). Posing as information technology personnel who

By the Numbers

$1.2 BILLION

The estimated amount of annual losses in the United States due to phishing attacks.

Cybercrime fighters will keep a watchful eye and develop new techniques for fighting cybercrime at this new high-tech center.

were seeking assistance to correct a network problem, security auditors telephoned one hundred IRS employees and managers. Of those who were called, thirty-five employees were convinced to reveal their login names and change their passwords to alternatives suggested by the callers. If this had been a real-world intrusion, hackers could have used that information to access confidential tax returns and personal financial data of millions of unsuspecting victims.

Other corporations, organizations, and agencies have performed their own tests to educate people about the risk of spearphishing attacks. In March 2005 New York's chief information security officer, William Pelgrin, designed a mock spearphishing program that he used with state government employees. Nearly ten thousand people received an e-mail with the logo of New York's Office of Cyber Security and Critical Infrastructure Coordination. The e-mail included the directive, "You are required to check your password by clicking on the link below and entering your password and email address by close of business today,"[69] and it directed employees to a special "password checker" Web site. About fifteen hundred of the recipients clicked on the link and tried to enter their passwords before the automated program stopped them from doing so. They received a follow-up note from Pelgrin with an explanation about the test, and a warning to not fall for such phishing tricks in the future.

A similar exercise was conducted in June 2004 with more than five hundred cadets at the U.S. Military Academy at West Point. The cadets received an e-mail from Colonel Robert Melville, who said he was writing to notify them of problems with their grades. They were ordered to click on a link to verify that their grades were correct, and more than 80 percent of the cadets did as they were instructed. They received a "gotcha!" e-mail informing them that there was no such officer as Robert Melville at West Point—it was a fictitious name. They were told that by clicking the link, they could have inadvertently downloaded spyware or other malicious software, and they were advised to be more careful in the future. Many of the cadets were not happy about being tricked, because they are taught to obey orders from officers, and that is what they thought they were doing. But according to Aaron Ferguson, a cybersecurity expert with the National Security Agency who teaches at West Point, such exercises are necessary because many cadets have been victims of real-life online fraud schemes.

Global Crime Rings

Exercises that educate people about spearphishing and other malicious acts are definitely valuable in helping to prevent cybercrime. Also, it is essential that computer users keep their systems protected with firewalls, spyware detection, antivirus software, and up-to-date security patches—yet surprisingly enough, many personal computer users and even large corporations fall short in this area. As savvy and malicious as criminal hackers have become, however, the most highly sophisticated security precautions are still not enough. "That's like a Band-Aid," says FBI agent Daniel J. Larkin. "If you don't try to take these guys down, they'll come back. You have to find a way to get to the live bodies and take them out at their roots. If you don't, you aren't solving the problem."[70]

One of the most challenging difficulties of catching computer hackers is that they do their dirty work from locations all over the world. They typically hang out in countries where hacking laws are either weak or nonexistent, and even when there are laws, they are not necessarily enforced. Hackers operating out of the United States may shelter their servers in China, Russia, or eastern Europe. This presents challenges because government officials in these parts of the world are not always cooperative with law enforcement officials from other countries. In 2000 the FBI tricked two Russian hackers into traveling to Seattle, Washington, by pretending to offer them jobs. When the two arrived, they were arrested, and agents later downloaded incriminating data from their computers (located in Russia) over the Internet. Two years later Russian officials filed charges against the FBI, saying that the downloads were illegal. Even though they did not follow through with the charges, Finnish security expert Mikko H. Hypponen

Hackers in India work in a cyber café. Foreign hackers form global crime rings to steal information from computers around the world.

says this lack of cooperation is commonplace with Russian authorities. He explains: "When you have a case that involves servers in Russia, you can almost hear the law-enforcement officials sigh."[71]

Because the Russian economy is suffering, hackers often write and sell malicious software in order to earn a living. According to security expert Eugene Kaspersky, many Russian hackers do not think they are doing anything criminal. They compare themselves to people who manufacture weapons: Even though they create the technology, they are not to blame for the harm it causes because they do not use it themselves. "In other words," writes journalist Bill Brenner, "they're not responsible if someone else is pulling the trigger."[72] Another factor is that hackers know there is little chance they will be pursued by Russian authorities because law enforcement of cybercrime in Russia is very weak.

One notorious Russian hacking gang is known as the HangUp Team, which freely commits cybercrimes—and gets away with one after another. For several years the gang has been releasing viruses such as Berbew and Webber, as well as the destructive Scob worm, which was designed to steal passwords and credit card numbers from users throughout the world. Gang members also rent out huge botnets to other hacker gangs who use them to spread viruses and spam e-mail. What is especially frustrating for American law enforcement is that the HangUp Team flaunts its criminal activities on the gang's Web site, and when they strike, they do not even try to cover their tracks. According to cybersecurity expert A. James Melnick, "These guys have set a new standard for sophistication among criminal hackers."[73]

Hacker Hunters

As daunting a task as catching criminal hackers is, law enforcement officials are ratcheting up their efforts to outsmart the bad guys and win the war on cybercrime. The goal of these "hacker hunters" is to infiltrate hacker groups, monitor

Catching a Hacker

For law enforcement officials, one of the most challenging parts of bringing a hacker to justice is obtaining and analyzing evidence that can be used in court. Such investigations are most often performed by certified computer forensic examiners and include the following basic steps:

1 The investigator makes sure that he or she is fully aware at all times where any items related to the investigation are located. A safe or cabinet is often used to secure items.

2 All relevant information is cataloged, including active, archival, and latent data. If possible, information that has been deleted is recovered, and encrypted, and password-protected data are identified. An exact copy of a hard drive image is made and authenticated against the original.

3 Additional sources of information are obtained, such as firewall logs, proxy and other server logs, and sign-in sheets.

4 The information is analyzed and interpreted to determine possible evidence. Both exculpatory (suspects did not do it) and inculpatory (they did it) evidence is sought out. If appropriate, encrypted files and password-protected files are cracked.

5 A written report is prepared and submitted with the investigator's findings and comments.

6 If necessary, the investigator provides expert witness testimony at a hacker's deposition, trial, or other legal proceeding.

their conversations on underground forums, and beat them at their own game. "Hackers used to believe there wasn't a law enforcement agency on their tail," says Larry Johnson of the U.S. Secret Service Criminal Investigative Division. "But for the last few years, the Secret Service and other agencies have directed a lot of resources to cybercrime, and we're starting to catch up."[74] Although investigative agencies such as the Secret Service, CIA, and FBI have been criticized in the past for not cooperating with each other, that is starting to change. In an effort to fight the growing problem of cybercrime, they are joining together to share information with each other and crack down on criminal hackers. The FBI, Secret Service, and other government agencies have formed more than fifty joint task forces that are located in cities throughout the United States, including Dallas, Chicago, Los Angeles, New York, New Orleans, and Salt Lake City.

The FBI has also built relationships with law enforcement organizations in other countries. In 2006 FBI agents traveled to Romania to take part in an operation known as Cardkeeper. The goal of the joint initiative was to break up a global identity theft ring that was responsible for major phishing attacks against financial institutions. Cardkeeper resulted in thirteen arrests, and it was so successful that the FBI decided to keep agents in Romania on a permanent basis. Today, there are more than 150 FBI agents stationed in sixty countries around the world, including Iraq and China.

The FBI's Cyber Action Teams (CATs) are composed of FBI agents, computer forensic analysts, and computer code experts. These small, highly trained teams travel all over the world, often leaving within hours of hearing about a cybercrime threat. In 2005 CATs were on their way to Turkey and Morocco with their computer forensics equipment within seventy-two hours of learning about the threat of the Zotob worm. They conducted an in-depth analysis and quickly identified the hackers. Then they furnished the information to Turkish and Moroccan law enforcement officials, who arrested Farid Essebar and Atilla Ekici fewer than eight days after the malicious software hit the Internet.

By the Numbers

15 MILLION

The estimated number of Americans who were victims of identity theft between 2005 and 2006.

Like the FBI, the Secret Service plays an integral role in the fight against cybercrime. One of its endeavors is the Electronics Crime Special Agent Program, also known as ECSAP. Approximately 160 men and women work as ECSAP agents. Most of them spent from three to eight years as Secret Service agents before they entered the specialized high-tech training program, and they are considered the crème de la crème of cybercrime investigators. They are naturally analytical and possess a combination of shrewd investigative abilities and law enforcement skills. "They're supercops," says security consultant Gerry Cavis, who was formerly a Secret Service agent himself. "They take the computer geek and the super investigator and create an agent who has unbelievable criminal investigative skills."[75] In addition to their initial training, ECSAP agents must keep their skills up to date by attending a three-week training session every year.

The ShadowCrew Takedown

One of ECSAP's greatest success stories was Operation Firewall, the nabbing of the infamous ShadowCrew hacking gang in October 2004. The operation was first launched in mid-2003. Within a few months, ECSAP agents had convinced a high-ranking ShadowCrew member to become an informant, which is a common technique in cybercrime investigations. Larry Johnson, special agent in charge of the Secret Service's Criminal Investigative Division, explains: "We utilize hackers because they know so much about other hackers. They speak the whole language of someone who's online 18 to 20 hours a day and lives off Red Bull."[76]

In August 2004 the informant helped ECSAP agents set up a new electronic "doorway" for gang members to enter the ShadowCrew Web site. He then spread the word, encouraging his fellow hackers to use the new gateway because it was a more secure way in and would provide greater anonymity. Members complied, which offered investigators an excellent opportunity to monitor all their online communications over

Omar Dhanani leaves the courthouse in 2005 after pleading guilty to crimes committed by the ShadowCrew and its Web site.

the following months. One gang member ECSAP agents observed was Omar Dhanani, a hacker from Fountain Valley, California, who used the screen name Voleur (French for "thief"). Dhanani often boasted on the forum that he could set up a special payment system for cybercrime transactions. Agents watched as he performed money-laundering services for ShadowCrew members in at least a dozen deals. They also observed numerous other transactions as members bought and sold stolen credit card numbers, user names and passwords, and other confidential information.

The online connection to ShadowCrew's Web site also helped ECSAP agents set up real-world stakeouts. First they subpoenaed records from Road Runner and other Internet service providers. Then they traced the IP addresses to houses and apartments in order to watch the gang members in person. One of their targets was a ShadowCrew hacker from Chicago named Rogerio Rodrigues, who was known online as Kerberos. ECSAP agents reported seeing him load a bulging bag of money into his vehicle and drive it to Citibank to make a deposit. They also observed him stopping at a Kinko's copy center, where they suspected he was picking up counterfeit merchandise.

On the evening of October 26, 2004, the ShadowCrew takedown was about to take place. By that time, ECSAP agents had gathered a monstrous load of evidence—almost two terabytes, which is about the same amount of information as one would find in an entire research library. Veteran Secret Service agent Brian K. Nagel, who was in charge of Operation Firewall, was waiting along with fifteen other agents in a command center in downtown Washington, D.C. To make sure that ShadowCrew members would be home at the time of the raid, the informant had called an online group meeting. At 9:00 P.M., Nagel gave the official "go" order. ECSAP agents, supported by local and international police in the United States and other countries, conducted a series of raids over a period of eight to ten hours. They arrested twenty-eight ShadowCrew members, most of whom were still at their computers. Later Nagel spoke about the success of Operation Firewall: "[Cybergangs] always thought they operated with anonymity. We rattled them."[77]

Fighting Identity Theft

ShadowCrew and other criminal hacking gangs are well known for the cybercrimes they commit, including identity theft. In a fact sheet released by the U.S. Department of Justice, identity theft was described as "a crime that victimizes people and businesses in every community from major cities to small towns, and robs victims of their individual freedoms."[78] To help fight the escalation of this serious crime, President George W. Bush established the nation's first Identity Theft Task Force in May 2006. Its goals are to improve and strengthen criminal prosecutions of identity theft, enhance data protection of confidential information that is maintained by the government and businesses, provide more comprehensive and effective guidance in avoiding identity theft to consumers and businesses, and improve methods of recovery and assistance for victims of identity theft. The task force is co-chaired by former attorney general Alberto Gonzalez and Federal Trade Commission Chairwoman Deborah Platt Majoras. Members include representatives

After speaking with victims of identity theft, President George W. Bush, center, announces the creation of the Identity Theft Task Force in 2006. It is the nation's first cybercrime task force.

from seventeen federal agencies and departments and were chosen based on areas of expertise that can contribute to the government's response to identity theft. Of the members, the FBI, the Secret Service, the Postal Inspection Service, and the Social Security Administrative Office of the Inspector General are empowered to investigate identity theft cases, while the Department of Justice prosecutes the cases.

In April 2007 the group presented Bush with a comprehensive strategic plan for combating identity theft. Majoras issued a statement about how the plan was designed to work: "Identity theft is a blight on America's privacy and security landscape. Identity thieves steal consumers' time, money, and security, just as sure as they steal their identifying information, and they cost businesses enormous sums. The Strategic Plan submitted to the President provides a blueprint for increased federal prevention and protection."[79] One of the task force's top recommendations was that the use of Social Security numbers by federal agencies be reduced, since these numbers are the most valuable commodity for identity thieves. The group also recommended the development of a broad public awareness campaign by federal agencies to educate people on ways to deter, detect, and defend against identity theft, as well as the formation of a National Identity Theft Law Enforcement Center. The center would serve as a clearinghouse for law enforcement agencies and help them coordinate their efforts and information, while also enabling them to investigate and prosecute identity thieves more efficiently and effectively.

The Dark Web Project

Although identity theft is a top priority of the federal government and law enforcement agencies, the threat of cyberterrorism is also an issue of great concern. According to Hsinchun Chen, increasing numbers of terrorist groups are using the Internet to spread propaganda, recruit new members, discuss how to make explosives, and plot attacks around the world.

Many terrorism-related Web sites are hidden inside other sites that are disguised so they do not look like the work of terrorists. Material is usually written in Arabic, but many other languages are also used, and some online forums include tens of thousands of members and a million postings.

Sifting through this enormous maze of data and making sense of it is a virtually impossible task for intelligence officials, yet it is extremely important in order to monitor online terrorist activities. To address this problem, Chen and a team of scientists from the Artificial Intelligence Lab at the University of Arizona created a giant searchable database called the Dark Web project. Its purpose is to uncover, cross-reference, catalog, and analyze all online content that is generated by terrorists throughout the world. Chen says that Dark Web is an excellent tool because it uses the power of advanced computers and applications to find patterns and connections that humans would not necessarily see. It has the capability to map terrorist networks, determine the importance of each member, and establish organizational hierarchies. It includes a powerful terrorism search engine with Web spiders that search discussion threads and other content to find where terrorist activities are taking place online.

Dark Web has already produced tangible results. Chen's team completed a study of online manuals and videos designed to help train terrorists to build and use improvised explosive devices, which are the roadside bombs that are often used against American soldiers in Iraq. The study also revealed where in the world the manuals are being downloaded. This kind of information can be invaluable to law enforcement professionals as they develop countermeasures to fight the war on terror.

Cybercrime in the Future

There is no doubt that fighting cyberterrorism, identity theft, malicious software attacks, and other crimes committed by hackers is a massive challenge. Law enforcement agencies and government officials are well aware of that, and they are stepping

Becoming a Computer Forensic Analyst

Job Description:

Often called "cybersleuths," computer forensic analysts follow the digital tracks left behind by hackers and other cybercriminals and gather evidence of their crimes. They often work with local, state, and federal law enforcement agencies, but they are also employed by large corporations and consulting firms. They search for evidence, often encrypted, that is hidden deep within computer systems.

Education:

Many computer forensic analysts learn much of what they know on the job, often starting in law enforcement careers and then going on to earn college degrees with computer security/forensics specialties. As the need for these professionals continues to grow, formal education is becoming more of a requirement.

Qualifications:

Certification is not usually required for computer forensic analysts, but they can benefit professionally by earning the Certified Information Systems Security Professional (CISSP) and the Certified Computer Examiner (CCE) designations.

Additional Information:

In addition to superior technical expertise and creativity, computer forensic analysts must be knowledgeable about the law, be able to create meticulous documentation, and be willing to work tirelessly toward accomplishing a goal.

Salary:

From $85,000 to more than $120,000 per year.

up efforts to stop cybercrime. They have made progress, and many hackers and criminal gangs have been brought to justice. But in spite of the progress that has been made, computer hacking is still a serious threat that is growing worse. Many hacking gurus—and even some law enforcement officials—believe there is no guaranteed way of putting a stop to it. Kevin Mitnick, the famed computer hacker, is one of them: "There is no technology that protects against [hacking]," he says. "You can sweep everyone under some sort of security policy, but it is really each individual [who exposes threats]. So anybody who interacts with computer-related equipment or even has access to a particular building can be targeted and exploited, so all the money that is spent on security is wasted. That's pretty scary."[80]

Notes

Introduction: "The Bad Guys Are Making a Lot of Money"

1. Melvyn Howe, "Boy Avoids Jail for Hacking into U.S. Weapons Lab," *Age*, February 4, 2004. www.theage.com.au/articles/2004/02/03/1075776059230.html.

2. Quoted in BBC News, "Teen Hacker Avoids Jail Sentence," February 2, 2004. http://news.bbc.co.uk/1/hi/technology/3452923.stm.

3. Quoted in Dan Verton, *Black Ice: The Invisible Threat of Cyber-Terrorism.* Emeryville, CA: McGraw-Hill/Osborne, 2003, p. ix.

4. Quoted in Jim Finkle, "Hackers Control PCs While Users Unaware," Reuters, September 21, 2007. www.reuters.com/article/internetNews/idUSN0923261120070921?feedType=RSS&feedName=internetNews.

Chapter 1: The Growing Threat of Cybercrime

5. Richard Stallman, "On Hacking," 2002. www.Stallman.org/articles/on-hacking.html.

6. Quoted in *PC World* staff, "The Digital Century: Software and the Internet," CNN, November 23, 1999. www.cnn.com/TECH/computing/9911/23/digital.century2.idg/index.html.

7. Quoted in Kevin Poulsen, "Feds Square Off with Organized Cyber Crime," *SecurityFocus*, February 17, 2005. www.securityfocus.com/news/10525.

8. Quoted in Byron Acohido and Jon Swartz, "Cybercrime Flourishes in Online Hacker Forums," *USA Today*, October 11, 2006. www.usatoday.com/tech/news/computersecurity/infotheft/2006-10-11-cybercrime-hacker-forums_x.htm.

9. Quoted in Thom Mrozek, "Romanian Charged with Hacking into U.S. Government Computers, Causing Nearly $1.5 Million in Losses," U.S. Attorney's Office news release, November 30, 2006. www.hq.nasa.gov/office/oig/hq/press/pr2007-C.pdf.

10. Acohido and Swartz, "Cybercrime Flourishes in Online Hacker Forums."

11. Federal Trade Commission, "About Identity Theft." www.ftc.gov/bcp/edu/microsites/idtheft/consumers/about-identity-theft.html.

12. Quoted in Byron Acohido, "SEC: 3 Traders Toyed with Google Options," *USA Today*, March 12, 2007. www.usatoday.com/tech/news/computersecurity/hacking/2007-03-12-cyber-scam-stocks_N.htm.

13. Quoted in U.S. Department of Justice, "ShadowCrew Organization Called 'One-Stop Online Marketplace for Identity Theft,'" October 28, 2004. www.usdoj.gov/criminal/cybercrime/mantovaniIndict.htm.

14. Quoted in Acohido and Swartz, "Cybercrime Flourishes in Online Hacker Forums."

15. Quoted in Jenn Abelson, "Breach of Data at TJX Is Called the Biggest Ever," *Boston Globe*, March 29, 2007. www.boston.com/business/globe/articles/2007/03/29/breach_of_data_at_tjx_is_called_the_biggest_ever.

16. Quoted in *Economist.com*, "A Walk on the Dark Side," August 30, 2007. www.economist.com/displaystory.cfm?story_id=9723768.

17. Quoted in John Swartz, "Security Experts: Rock Phish Is Behind Growing 'Net Fraud," *USA Today*, October 10, 2007. www.usatoday.com/money/industries/technology/2007-10-10-rock-fish_N.htm.

18. Quoted in Thomas Claburn, "FBI Arrests Bot Masters as Cyber Crime Worsens," *Information Week*, November 29, 2007. www.informationweek.com/security/showArticle.jhtml?articleID=204301293.

Chapter 2: "It Was Like a Game"

19. Hugo Cornwall, *The Hacker's Handbook*. London: Century Communications, 1985. www.textfiles.com/etext/MODERN/hhbk.

20. Quoted in Jon Ronson, "Game Over," *Guardian Unlimited*, July 9, 2005. www.guardian.co.uk/weekend/story/0,,1523143,00.html.

21. Quoted in Ronson, "Game Over."

22. Quoted in Nigel Watson, "'UFO Hacker' Tells What He Found," *Wired*, June 21, 2006. www.wired.com/techbiz/it/news/2006/06/71182.

23. Quoted in Clark Boyd, "Profile: Gary McKinnon," BBC News, April 3, 2007. http://news.bbc.co.uk/2/hi/technology/4715612.stm.

24. Quoted in Thomas C. Greene, "Chapter One: Kevin Mitnick's Story," The Register, January 13, 2003. www.theregister.co.uk/2003/01/13/chapter_one_kevin_mitnicks_story.

25. Quoted in Greene, "Chapter One."

26. Quoted in Greene, "Chapter One."

27. Quoted in CNN.com, "A Convicted Hacker Debunks Some Myths," October 7, 2005. www.cnn.com/2005/TECH/internet/10/07/kevin.mitnick.cnna.

28. Dan Verton, *The Hacker Diaries: Confessions of Teenage Hackers.* Berkeley, CA: McGraw-Hill/Osborne, 2002, p. 69.

29. Verton, *The Hacker Diaries*, p. 70.

30. Quoted in Matt Richtel, "Canada Arrests 15-Year-Old in Web Attack," *New York Times*, April 20, 2000. http://query.nytimes.com/gst/fullpage.html?res=9F04E0DC1131F933A15757C0A9669C8B63&n=Top/News/Business/Companies/eBay%20Inc.

31. Quoted in Jaclyn Perrelli, "Hacking's Boy Wonder," *PC Magazine*, August 21, 2007, p. 18.

32. Quoted in PBS Frontline "Hackers: Interview: Anonymous," February 2001. www.pbs.org/wgbh/pages/frontline/shows/hackers/interviews/anon.html.

Chapter 3: Malicious Software

33. Quoted in The Mac Security Blog, "Happy Birthday Computer Viruses!" September 14, 2007. http://blog.intego.com/2007/09/14/happy-birthday-computer-viruses.

34. *Network Security Journal*, "New Hacker Tactics Unveiled," September 25, 2006. www.networksecurityjournal.com/features/new-hacker-tactics-unveiled-092506.

35. Quoted in Sharon Gaudin, "McAfee's DeWalt Pushes for Legislation to Battle Cyber Criminals," *Information Week*, July 19, 2007. www.informationweek.com/news/showArticle.jhtml?articleID=201002319.

36. Quoted in Sophos News, "Don't Download Microsoft Security Bulletin MS07-0065!" June 27, 2007. www.sophos.com/pressoffice/news/articles/2007/06/bogusmspatch.html.

37. Quoted in Will Knight, "Malicious Software Turns PSP into a 'Brick,'" NewScientistTech, October 7, 2005. http://technology.newscientist.com/channel/tech/electronic-threats/dn8116-malicious-software-turns-psp-into-a-brick.html.

38. Quoted in Sophos News, "Hacker Pleads Guilty to Spreading IRC Trojan Horse," February 22, 2007. www.sophos.com/pressoffice/news/articles/2007/02/honour.html.

39. Kim Zetter, "How a Computer Virus Works," CNN.com Technology, October 23, 2000. http://archives.cnn.com/2000/TECH/computing/10/23/virus.works.idg.

40. Quoted in Will Sturgeon, "Sasser Virus Writer Admits Guilt in Trial," Silicon.com, July 5, 2005. http://software.silicon.com/security/0,39024655,39150056,00.htm.

41. Brian Krebs, "Invasion of the Computer Snatchers," *Washington Post*, February 19, 2006, p. W10.

42. Quoted in Byron Acohido and Jon Swartz, "Malicious-Software Spreaders Get Sneakier, More Prevalent," *USA Today*, April 23, 2006. www.usatoday.com/tech/news/computersecurity/infotheft/2006-04-23-bot-herders_x.htm.

43. Quoted in Matt Chapman, "Second Monster Hack Affects Millions," VNUNet.com, August 30, 2007. www.vnunet.com/vnunet/news/2197659/second-monster-hack-affects.

44. Quoted in "Super Bowl Fuels Gambling Sites' Extortion Fears," *IT World Security*, January 28, 2004. http://security.itworld.com/4339/040128gamblingsites/page_1.html.

45. Quoted in Acohido and Swartz, "Malicious-Software Spreaders Get Sneakier, More Prevalent."

46. Federal Bureau of Investigation, "The Case of the 'Zombie King,'" May 8, 2006. www.fbi.gov/page2/may06/botnet050806.htm.

47. Quoted in Brian Krebs, "Botmaster Sentenced to 57 Months in Prison," Washington Post Security Fix blog, May 8, 2006. http://blog.washingtonpost.com/securityfix/2006/05/botmaster_sentenced_to.html.

Chapter 4: Cyberterrorism

48. Quoted in Gabriel Weimann, "Cyberterrorism: How Real Is the Threat?" U.S. Institute of Peace, December 2004. www.usip.org/pubs/specialreports/sr119.html.

49. Joshua Green, "The Myth of Cyberterrorism," *Washington Monthly*, November 2002. www.washingtonmonthly.com/features/2001/0211.green.html.

50. Quoted in Breanne Wagner, "Electronic Jihad: Experts Downplay Imminent Threat of Cyberterrorism," *National Defense*, July 2007. www.nationaldefensemagazine.org/issues/2007/July/ExpertsDownplay.htm.

51. Dan Verton, *Black Ice: The Invisible Threat of Cyber-Terrorism*. Emeryville, CA: McGraw-Hill/Osborne, 2003, p. 82.

52. Quoted in Senator Charles E. Schumer, "Schumer: New York Dangerously Unprepared for Cyber Terrorist Attack," press release, February 17, 2002. www.senate.gov/~schumer/SchumerWebsite/pressroom/press_releases/PR00844.html.

53. Quoted in Green, "The Myth of Cyberterrorism."

54. George Mason University School of Law, "Critical Infrastructure Protection Program: What Is CIP?" http://cipp.gmu.edu/cip.

55. Weimann, "Cyberterrorism."

56. President George W. Bush, "Critical Infrastructure Identification, Prioritization, and Protection," White House press release, December 17, 2003. www.whitehouse.gov/news/releases/2003/12/20031217-5.html.

57. Verton, *Black Ice*, p. xxiii.

58. Quoted in Robert Lemos, "Safety: Assessing the Infrastructure Risk," CNET News.com, August 26, 2002. www.news.com/2009-1001-954780.html.

59. Quoted in Steven Kotler, "'Dark Web' Project Takes on Cyber-Terrorism," FOX News, October 12, 2007. www.foxnews.com/story/0,2933,300956,00.html.

60. Quoted in Laura Blumenfeld, "Dissertation Could Be Security Threat," *Washington Post*, July 8, 2003. www.washingtonpost.com/ac2/wp-dyn/A23689-2003Jul7.

61. Keith Lourdeau, "Virtual Threat, Real Terror: Cyberterrorism in the 21st Century," GlobalSecurity.org, February 24, 2004. www.globalsecurity.org/security/library/congress/2004_h/040224-lourdeau.htm.

62. Quoted in PBS *Frontline*, "Interview: Hacker," April 23, 2003. www.pbs.org/wgbh/pages/frontline/shows/cyberwar/interviews/hacker.html.

63. Quoted in Jeanne Meserve, "Sources: Staged Cyber Attack Reveals Vulnerability in Power Grid," CNN.com, September 26, 2007. www.cnn.com/2007/US/09/26/power.at.risk/#cnnSTCText.

64. Todd Datz, "Out of Control," *CSO*, August 2004. www.csoonline.com/read/080104/control.html.

65. Quoted in Verton, *Black Ice*, p. xxv.

Chapter 5: Can Computer Hackers Be Stopped?

66. Dave DeWalt, *McAfee Virtual Criminology Report*, November 2007. www.mcafee.com/us/local_content/reports/mcafee_criminology_report2007_en.pdf.

67. Jack Blaisdale, interview with the author, October 18, 2007.

68. Blaisdale interview.

69. Quoted in David Bank, "'Spear Phishing' Tests Educate People About Online Scams," *Wall Street Journal*, August 17, 2005. http://online.wsj.com/public/article/SB112424042313615131-z_8jLB2WkfcVtgdAWf6LRh733sg_20060817.html.

70. Quoted in Brian Grow, "Hacker Hunters," *Business Week*, May 30, 2005. http://yahoo.businessweek.com/magazine/content/05_22/b3935001_mz001.htm.

71. Quoted in Grow, "Hacker Hunters."

72. Bill Brenner, "How Russia Became a Malware Hornet's Nest," SearchSecurity.com, October 9, 2007. http://searchsecurity.techtarget.com/originalContent/0,289142,sid14_gci1275987,00.html?asrc=SS_CLA_299990&psrc=CLT_14.

73. Quoted in Grow, "Hacker Hunters."

74. Quoted in Alan Joch, "Super Cops," *FedTech Magazine*, August 2005. www.fedtechmagazine.com/article.asp?item_id=127.

75. Quoted in Joch, "Super Cops."

76. Quoted in Joch, "Super Cops."

77. Quoted in Grow, "Hacker Hunters."

78. U.S. Department of Justice, "Fact Sheet: The Work of the President's Identity Theft Task Force," September 19, 2006. www.ftc.gov/os/2006/09/060919IDtheftfactsheet.pdf.

79. Quoted in U.S. Securities and Exchange Commission, "The President's Identity Theft Task Force Releases Comprehensive Strategic Plan to Combat Identity Theft," April 23, 2007. www.sec.gov/news/press/2007/2007-69.htm.

80. Quoted in John Brandon, "Q&A with the Forefather of Hacking," *PC Magazine*, August 23, 2007. www.pcmag.com/article2/0,1759,2174605,00.asp.

Glossary

bandwidth: A measure of the amount of data that can be sent over a network connection during a certain period of time (usually measured in bits per second).

botnet: Created from the words *robot* and *network*, a botnet is a collection of computers that have been infected with malicious software and are controlled remotely by hackers.

critical infrastructure: The complex, interdependent systems, networks, and assets that serve large populations throughout developed countries.

cyberterrorism: The use of the Internet to perform terrorist acts.

distributed denial of service (DDoS) attack: An attack whereby a computer or network is bombarded with meaningless data in an attempt to cause it to become overloaded and crash.

identity theft: The crime of stealing personal information (such as Social Security numbers) in order to impersonate someone and perform fraudulent acts.

malware: Malicious software, such as computer viruses, worms, and Trojan horses.

phishing: A form of Internet fraud that aims to steal confidential information such as user names, passwords, credit card numbers, Social Security numbers, and bank account information.

social engineering: Deceptive techniques that are used to manipulate people into performing certain actions or divulging confidential information.

spyware: Software that secretly gathers information about user behavior on the Internet.

Trojan horse: A term that describes a set of malicious instructions hidden inside a program that tell the program what to do.

virus: A type of malware that is "contagious," much like a communicable disease, and is designed to spread to other computers by infecting them with a copy of itself.

worm: A malicious program that is designed to spread itself by exploiting existing bugs in software.

For More Information

Books

Jon Erickson, *Hacking: The Art of Exploitation*. San Francisco: No Starch, 2007. A comprehensive and interesting book about the methods used by tech-savvy hackers, including how they view hacking: as creative problem solving.

Ankit Fadia, *Unofficial Guide to Ethical Hacking*. Boston: Thomson Course Technology, 2006. A great book for anyone who is interested in how computer hackers are different from crackers, including how true hackers can help protect computer systems from criminals.

Kevin D. Mitnick, *The Art of Intrusion: The Real Stories Behind the Exploits of Hackers, Intruders, and Deceivers*. Indianapolis: Wiley, 2005. Written by one of the most famous computer hackers of all time, this book tells the story of a criminal turned white hat hacker.

Dan Verton, *Black Ice: The Invisible Threat of Cyber-Terrorism*. Emeryville, CA: McGraw-Hill/Osborne, 2003. Verton, who is a veteran investigative reporter as well as author, provides a blunt, and chilling, account of the real threat of cyberterrorism.

———, *The Hacker Diaries: Confessions of Teenage Hackers*. Berkeley, CA: McGraw-Hill/Osborne, 2002. An insightful book that provides a glimpse into the minds of teenage tech-whizzes who learned the art of hacking.

Periodicals

Robert Lemos, "Hacking for Dollars," *PC Magazine*, December 26, 2006. Discusses how malicious code has become more sophisticated and is now a key element in the growth of online crime.

Jaclyn Perrelli, "Hacking's Boy Wonder," *PC Magazine*, August 21, 2007. The focus of this article is Jonathan "c0mrade" James, who, at the age of fifteen, hacked into the Pentagon's and NASA's computer systems in 1999 and became the youngest person to be imprisoned under the U.S. federal cybercrime law.

Internet Sources

Byron Acohido and Jon Swartz, "Malicious-Software Spreaders Get Sneakier, More Prevalent," *USA Today*, April 23, 2006. www.usatoday.com/tech/news/computer security/infotheft/2006-04-23-bot-herders_x.htm. A story about the growing threat of malicious software that is created by criminals who want to steal confidential information through bot networks.

Marilyn Elias, "Most Teen Hackers More Curious than Criminal," *USA Today*,

August 19, 2007. www.usatoday.com/
news/health/2007-08-19-teen-hackers_
N.htm. Interesting story about a survey to
determine why kids hack into computers;
nine out of ten said that they do it because
it is exciting or challenging, rather than to
cause any harm.

Mike McGuff, "Former Teen Hacker Has a
Warning for Parents," ABC12.com, April
12, 2007. http://abclocal.go.com/wjrt/
story?section=sci_tech&id=5194430. An
article about Houston teenager Steven
Nick, who used his hacking skills to
disable parental software on his friends'
computers and now uses that experience
to educate parents about keeping their
kids safe on the Internet.

Breanne Wagner, "Electronic Jihad:
Experts Downplay Imminent Threat of
Cyberterrorism," National Defense, July
2007. www.nationaldefensemagazine.
org/issues/2007/July/ExpertsDownplay.
htm. An informative article about cyberterrorism, including various expert view-
points about the possibility that it could
occur.

Peter Warren, "School for Scoundrels,
Guardian, October 6, 2005. www.guardian.
co.uk/technology/2005/oct/06/hacking.
internetcrime. The author writes about
his experience at an elite school in the
United Kingdom that educates computer security experts on how to protect
against hackers by teaching how hackers
think.

Web Sites

**Computer Crime and Intellectual Property
Section, U.S. Department of Justice**
(www.cybercrime.gov). Includes a collection of current press releases about
computer security and cybercrime, a "hot
documents" section with downloadable
publications, and links to other good resources.

**Federal Bureau of Investigation (FBI)
Cyber Investigations** (www.fbi.gov/
cyberinvest/cyberhome.htm). Includes a
wealth of information about computer
crime, including statistics, FBI task forces,
programs, and news articles.

How Stuff Works (www.howstuffworks.
com). This site includes various articles
of interest about computer hacking, including the hacker culture, the motivation
for hacking, laws against hacking, and
how hackers attack computer systems,
and includes profiles of some of the most
famous hackers. There are also a number
of good articles and a section titled "How
Computer Viruses Work."

Index

Picture Credits

About the Author

Peggy J. Parks holds a bachelor of science degree from Aquinas College in Grand Rapids, Michigan, where she graduated magna cum laude. She is a freelance author who has written more than sixty nonfiction educational books for children and young adults, as well as self-publishing her own cookbook titled *Welcome Home: Recipes, Memories, and Traditions from the Heart*. Parks lives in Muskegon, Michigan, a town that she says inspires her writing because of its location on the shores of Lake Michigan.